A Journey of Self-Discovery and Redemption

FORGIVING WHAT I CANNOT FORGET

RISING FROM THE SHADOWS

TEKEISHA LEE

ISBN:979-8-218-43260-7 (Paperback)

ISBN: 979-8-218-45901-7 (Hardcover)

Library of Congress Control Number: 202491099

Book Designed & Published by Dara Publishing

Place of Publication: Horn Lake. Mississippi

Printed in the United States of America.

Disclaimer: The publisher and the authors do not make any guarantee or other promise as to any results that may be obtained from using the content of this book. This publication is meant as a source of valuable information for the reader; however, it is not meant as a substitute for direct expert assistance. If such a level of assistance is required, the services of a competent professional should be sought.

Dedication

*First and foremost, I dedicate this work to God. Thank you!
Your constant presence has been my guiding light over the
years. Your faithfulness has brightened my path and led me to
discover my true purpose. Through your divine intervention, I
found the strength to overcome procrastination and complete
this book. In my weakest moments, I couldn't have imagined
reaching this point without your help. I am eternally grateful
to you, and I pray that this book inspires others, drawing them
closer to Christ.*

*To my parents and siblings, I want to express my deep love for
each of you. I know my journey with Christ might have seemed
unconventional initially. But I hope you, too, will experience
His transformative presence in your lives, just as I have. His
love is profound, and I want you all to know
He deeply loves you.*

Table of Contents

Introduction

Finding Light in the Darkest Hours 9

Chapter 1

The Insidious Grip of Emotional Abuse 21

Chapter 2

Breaking Free from the Chains of Abuse 31

Chapter 3

Cruel Revelation 41

Chapter 4

Shattered Trust 51

Chapter 5

Scars of Love 59

Chapter 6

Almost Lost My Mind 69

Chapter 7

Betrayal and Redemption 79

Chapter 8

The Rebound Person 91

Chapter 9

From Brokenness to Hope 99

Chapter 10

A Work In Progress 109

Chapter 11

A Full Circle Moment 117

Chapter 12

Embracing Redemption and Resilience 123

About the Author 129

Acknowledgement 131

Crisis Hotline Information... 135

Thank You 139

FINDING LIGHT IN THE DARKEST HOURS

Life, as we know it, is woven from experiences, each one shaping who we are. Every person has a unique story, filled with joy, sadness, and a continuous search for meaning, healing, and growth.

As you hold this book, understand that I'm not a famous expert or a celebrity with all the answers. Instead, I'm just like you, traveling through life, hoping to share parts of my journey that might connect with yours and offer some comfort.

This book is a memoir, a self-help memoir, where I lay out the honest details of my life. It tells how I fell into deep despair, wandered through great pain, made plenty of mistakes, and eventually found my way to healing and redemption. It's a story about bouncing back, finding hope, and realizing that we all have the power to shape our futures.

My story starts with a simple childhood, growing up in a setting that was often tougher than nurturing. I dealt with the same fears, insecurities, and hopes that many of you might find familiar. I didn't come from a privileged background, but I was lucky to have a family that did everything they could to support me.

Back then, life was simple, and I was blissfully unaware of the challenges ahead. My early years were joyful, filled with the love of my parents and what seemed like endless possibilities. But as we often hear, change is the only constant, and my life was no exception.

As I grew older, the skies of my childhood became overcast, and I faced trials that tested my strength. I encountered pain and adversity, each event gradually wearing down the innocence of my youth and weakening my once-strong spirit. In the following chapters, I'll share some of the toughest moments of my life, including deep losses, heartbreaking disappointments, and a series of bad decisions.

It's important to remember that adversity is something that connects all of us. It doesn't care about boundaries, status, or who you are. In sharing my struggles, I want you to realize that you're not alone. The pain and the challenges you face are shared by many, binding us together. By telling you about my experiences, I hope you find some comfort in knowing that others have faced similar troubles and come out stronger and wiser.

In the next chapters, I'll take you through the maze of my poor decisions, the dark times when I lost my way, failed relationships, and the shadows of my past that followed me. However, it was in these darkest moments that I started to look for light. My story isn't here to shock you; it's a testament to our resilience as humans. It's a reminder that no matter how far you've fallen, there's always a way back to the light.

Everyone reaches a turning point in life, that moment when you choose whether to give in to your circumstances or overcome them. My turning point was both heartbreaking and life-changing. And I share that pivotal experience in this book, hoping it inspires you to find your own moments of courage.

This memoir is designed to help transform and heal. We'll explore healing practices, coping mechanisms, and the insights that helped me take back my life and discover my inner strength. It's about finding hope, confronting our fears, and triumphing over them. This book is a celebration of our ability to rewrite our life stories.

By sharing my journey, I reach out to you, offering the knowledge that you, too, can overcome the shadows. We all have the potential to find light and move toward healing, redemption, and a brighter future. Through these pages, you'll see that even in the darkest times, there's always a glimmer of hope. By the end of this book, I hope to leave you believing that you control your narrative, your past doesn't define your future, and you have the strength to rise above adversity.

So, as we begin this journey together, I invite you to walk with me, page by page, as I share my past mistakes and the victories that came from overcoming them. But first, there are a few things you need to understand.

Recognizing the Chains of Deceit

A journey of healing often starts with recognizing the chains that bind us. For those who have endured emotional abuse, this realization comes slowly as we understand that those we loved and trusted might have misled us. It's a painful process involving denial, shame, and the destruction of beliefs we once held sacred. The truth gradually makes its presence felt, perhaps through subtle lies we accept as truths or the pain of recalling broken promises. Bit by bit, we piece together the shards of our broken trust, and it becomes clear—we have been emotionally abused.

Recognizing these chains isn't a momentary event but a series of revelations, each bringing us closer to accepting the truth. It happens in quiet moments when we doubt our value or cry out the pain we can no longer hide. It's when we look in the mirror and see not only our reflection but also the scars of deception.

Reflecting on my own experiences, I see that acknowledging abuse was both incredibly hard and absolutely vital. I often wondered, "Why me?" But in those dark times, perhaps a more fitting question was, "Why not me?" This doesn't place blame but rather accepts the harsh truth that abuse can happen to anyone.

For many, the descent into abuse is gradual and nearly imperceptible. It might start with small things we excuse as misunderstandings or just stress. But over time, these minor issues can evolve into a suffocating mesh of manipulation and control.

Breaking free requires immense courage and strength. It involves facing our deepest fears and admitting that our situation is neither normal nor acceptable. It's akin to walking out of a fog and into the light, where the reality of our circumstances becomes undeniably clear.

Breaking Free: The Courage to Let Go

Once we see the deceit for what it is, the next step is finding the bravery to break free. This isn't an easy decision. Letting go of the things we believe in can feel like losing part of who we are. Yet, staying in a toxic relationship becomes too painful, slowly eating away at our self-worth.

Breaking free takes a lot of strength. It starts with a quiet determination that grows inside us, a little spark of self-love that won't go out. It happens when we find the courage to walk away, to leave behind the lies and empty promises. It's in the shaky hands that reach out for help, looking for safety in new places.

The journey to freedom isn't easy. There are times when we doubt if we're doing the right thing. Fears hold us tight, trying to pull us back into old, harmful patterns. But with each step forward, we remind ourselves of our worth and our right to a life free from emotional abuse.

Seeking Support: Finding Strength in Community

After breaking free, we often find ourselves adrift, lost in a sea of confusion and pain. This is when the value of support becomes clear. Whether it's from friends, family, support groups, or therapists, having someone to rely on can make a huge difference.

Support can take many forms. It might be a friend who listens without judgment, a counselor who guides us through the maze of our emotions, or a support group where we find comfort in shared experiences. It's realizing that we are not alone and that others have faced similar struggles and have come out stronger.

Seeking support isn't a sign of weakness but a mark of strength. It requires bravery to reach out and admit that we can't do this by ourselves. It's the first step towards healing, a lifeline in the turbulent recovery journey.

Confronting Emotional Scars: The Road to Self-Rediscovery

Healing from emotional abuse isn't a straight path. It's more like a rollercoaster of emotions, with highs and lows. Confronting our emotional wounds means dealing with the pain directly, allowing ourselves to fully experience what we've been through.

It's okay to feel angry, grieve the lost trust, and mourn the person we were before the deceit. It's okay to cry, scream into the void, and rage against the unfairness of it all. Healing can be messy, unpredictable, and painful. But it's also freeing, a chance to let go of old illusions and discover new aspects of ourselves.

As we deal with our emotional wounds, we learn to forgive— not for the people who hurt us, but for ourselves. Forgiveness isn't about excusing what they did but letting go of their grip on our hearts. It's a powerful act of self-love, a way to take back our power.

Rebuilding Trust: Learning to Believe in Ourselves Again

One of the harshest realities of emotional abuse is how it breaks our trust in ourselves. When those we loved and trusted betray us, we naturally become cautious and question our decisions.

Rebuilding trust is a gentle process. It involves learning to tell the difference between truth and lies and recognizing real love versus manipulation. It means taking small steps and carefully testing the waters before fully diving in. It's about recognizing that we deserve love and respect and that kindness should be a standard in our interactions.

Trust is a valuable gift we give ourselves. It's the belief in our resilience and ability to rise above even the deepest betrayals. It's a slow process, a gradual opening of our hearts to new possibilities of self-discovery and renewal.

Rediscovering Identity and Purpose and the Journey Within

As we navigate the healing process, something extraordinary begins to unfold. We start to rediscover ourselves—the person we were before the deceit and the person we are evolving into afterward. It feels like a rebirth, peeling away old layers to reveal the resilient core beneath.

We find our passions again, the activities that used to bring us joy before they were overshadowed by deceit. We tap into our strengths, the inner reserves of courage and resilience that helped us endure the toughest times. We also revive our dreams, the ambitions we thought were swept away by betrayal.

In this process of rediscovery, we find a new purpose. We become advocates for ourselves and for others who have suffered similar betrayals. We use our voices to speak out against emotional abuse, to raise awareness, and to offer hope to those still struggling with heartbreak.

Through our healing journey, we transform into phoenixes rising from the ashes—stronger, wiser, and more compassionate. Our scars become symbols of our resilience, and our voices are a source of hope for those still navigating their way out of the darkness.

Forgiving What I Cannot Forget :Rising from the Shadows - A Journey of Self-Discovery and Redemption is a book crafted for survivors of abuse ,for those who have been deceived and betrayed in relationships ,for individuals coping with the aftermath of heartbreak ,and for anyone seeking hope and resilience in overcoming adversity.

My mission and purpose of this book:

- To provide comfort and support to survivors of abuse, deceit, and heartbreak.

- To offer guidance and insights on how to navigate the complexities of healing and self-discovery.

- To share personal stories to inspire hope and resilience in challenging times.

- To illuminate the role of faith and belief in overcoming life's trials.

Abuse, deceit, and heartbreak may have left their scars, but they do not define us. Through recognition, breaking free, seeking support, confronting emotional scars, rebuilding trust, and rediscovering identity and purpose, we embark on a journey of healing—a journey from heartbreak to renewal to redemption.

Note from the Author

Dear Reader,

I'm excited to share with you a glimpse into my personal journey through the ten deeply personal stories that shape this book. These stories are not just mine—they reflect experiences many have endured on the path of abuse, deceit, and heartbreak.

In these narratives, I reveal my own mistakes, the toxic relationships that ensnared me, and the dark moments that nearly overwhelmed me. Each tale delves into the complexities of human relationships, our inherent vulnerabilities, and the resilience that we all possess.

The reason for sharing these stories is deeply personal and serves a dual purpose. Firstly, they act as a mirror for those who have faced similar challenges. By opening up about my experiences, I hope to offer comfort and validation to those who have felt isolated in their struggles. You may see reflections of your own experiences in these pages, moments that echo your personal journey.

Secondly, these stories underscore the potential for redemption and growth. They remind us that no matter how severe our wounds, how complicated our relationships, or how dark our situations are, there is always a way forward. Through self-reflection, forgiveness, and a readiness to face our truths, we can step out of the shadows and into the light of self-discovery, navigating through both joy and sorrow, triumph and defeat.

Through my words, I aim to illuminate your path with the light of hope and faith, reassuring you that even in the darkest nights, hope persists. As you turn these pages, may you find comfort in knowing you are not alone. Discover the strength of resilience in adversity, the beauty of love in brokenness, and the constant grace of God in every chapter of your life. Allow these stories to move, challenge, and inspire you. Let this book be your companion on your journey, a source of comfort when you need it, and a beacon of hope in your darker moments.

"Trust in the Lord with all your heart and lean not on your own understanding; in all your ways submit to him, and he will make your paths straight" ~ Proverbs 3:5-6

This scripture offers a timeless truth that resonates deeply within us. It encourages us to release our grip on control and to surrender our worries and uncertainties to the Almighty.

As you read, I invite you to reflect on these words. Let them guide you, especially when your path seems uncertain. Trust in God's plan, even in moments when you feel surrounded by darkness. When we yield to His will, He will undoubtedly clear our way. Thank you for accompanying me on this journey.

With love and gratitude,

Tekeisha Lee

Chapter 1

THE INSIDIOUS GRIP OF EMOTIONAL ABUSE

Emotional abuse is a hidden, damaging force that often goes unnoticed, gradually undermining one's self-esteem and leaving unseen scars on the mind. As someone who has survived this kind of trauma in my relationships, I can speak to its devastating impact. The tactics used—manipulation, gaslighting, constant belittling— are designed to weaken the victim's spirit, making them dependent on and easily controlled by the abuser.

This type of abuse can occur in any relationship, whether romantic, familial, or platonic, and its perpetrators come from all backgrounds, often masking their harmful behavior with feigned love or concern. It starts subtly, with small comments or actions that sow seeds of doubt. Over time, these seeds grow, leading to intense self-loathing and a distorted sense of reality.

For many, recognizing that they are experiencing emotional abuse is difficult, filled with denial, rationalizations, and fear of loneliness. I found myself justifying the warning signs, telling myself that the emotional distance, insults, and constant need for validation were just temporary troubles common to any relationship.

However, through research and personal reflection, I realized the harsh truth: emotional abuse is a method of control, systematically breaking down one's independence and self-worth. The abuser's aim is to foster fear and dependence, warping the victim's reality so that their identity becomes deeply entwined with the whims of the abuser.

Rebuilding skills like setting boundaries, creating a support network, and trusting one's intuition—abilities often diminished by emotional abuse—is crucial. Additionally, understanding the dynamics of trauma bonding, which can bind victims to their abusers despite clear signs of harm, is vital.

Embarking on a path of self-love and compassion is key to healing. For too long, I measured my worth by others' standards, seeking approval and acceptance from outside sources, which set me up for further harm. It was only when I began a journey of radical self-acceptance that I started to truly heal, breaking free from the chains of emotional abuse and regaining my strength.

The Echoes of Trauma

Reflecting on the path that led me to this pivotal moment, I think about the echoes that resound in our hearts—echoes that can either confine us or drive us toward freedom. For many, the roots of emotional turmoil were planted well before we ventured into romantic relationships, rooted deep in our childhood experiences.

My story mirrors this. The little girl who once danced freely, her laughter ringing with pure joy, gradually receded as shadows of hardship appeared. The once-clear skies clouded over me, and I faced trials that tested my spirit's resilience.

You might also remember times when the simplicity of childhood was eroded, replaced by a burden that weighed heavily on your soul. Profound losses, deep disappointments, and voices whispering you were "not enough," or witnessing the divorce of your parents or violence at home—such experiences leave lasting marks that shape how we see ourselves and the world.

During these early years, I first faced what I would later understand as emotional abuse. The whispers of self-doubt, the subtle erosion of my self-esteem, and the constant search for validation were the seeds that later blossomed into the toxic relationships of my adult life.

As I moved through adolescence and into young adulthood, those traumatic echoes grew louder, influencing every part of my life. I found myself drawn to partners who reflected the painful dynamics I had known, seeking out the familiarity of chaos subconsciously.

The cycle of emotional abuse is cunning, slipping into our lives stealthily, robbing us of our self-worth, and making us question our reality. It shows up in gaslighting, where our experiences are twisted, making us doubt our perceptions. It manifests in manipulation, slowly wearing down our boundaries and stripping away our independence, piece by piece.

For those who have been through such trauma, the journey to healing can feel overwhelming. The impact of abuse is so deep that it becomes part of our inner voice, feeding us self-doubt and continuing the harmful cycles that have hurt us so much.

However, it's during these tough times that we need to muster the courage to face our demons and expose the dark corners that have trapped us for too long. I can tell you that this path demands a lot of self-kindness and a readiness to forgive ourselves for our decisions when we were hurting.

By addressing these echoes from our past, we can truly heal and build a future where trauma no longer steers our lives.

These personal stories will give you a close look at how abuse affected me—from the subtle emotional manipulation that slowly wore down my self-esteem to the severe physical violence that left both visible and invisible scars and the profound betrayal that occurred as my trust was shattered over and over. Yet, even in the depths of my suffering, you'll find glimmers of hope that sustained me, moments of clarity that reassured me I wasn't defined by my trauma. Instead, I discovered the courage to overcome it, strengthened by my faith in God and my love for my children, who were my support pillars.

As you dive into these candid reflections from my life, you might see reflections of your own experiences in the universal truths that connect us all as survivors. The feelings of being alone, the struggle with self-love, the creeping self-doubt, and the intense yearning to regain the joy and authenticity that used to come so naturally to me from my childhood into adulthood. Through this shared understanding, I hope you find comfort, a reminder that you're not alone in your fight and that your experiences, no matter how tough, are valid and deserve to be shared.

My stories across various relationships are not just warnings; they are signals of hope, showing the way I moved towards healing, self-love, and taking back my power.

Activity

Healing Exercise - Reflective Writing and Healing Circle

Objective:

Today, I invite you on a deeply personal journey of reflection and healing. Find a quiet, comfortable space where you can fully immerse yourself in this experience without any interruptions.

Materials Needed:

1. Writing materials (notebook, journal, or computer)

2. Comfortable and quiet space

Instructions:

1. Setting the Scene:

- Find a quiet and comfortable space where you feel safe and relaxed.

- Set aside dedicated time for this activity, ensuring that you won't be interrupted.

2. Reflective Writing:

- Begin by taking a few deep breaths to center yourself and create a sense of calm.

- Open your notebook, journal, or computer and start writing freely about your experiences of emotional abuse.

- Write without judgment or censorship, allowing your thoughts and emotions to flow onto the page.

- Reflect on specific instances of emotional abuse you have experienced, the impact it has had on your self-esteem, and any patterns or echoes of trauma that you recognize in your life.

- Consider how these experiences have shaped your perceptions of yourself, your relationships, and the world around you.

3. Digging Deeper:

- As you write, delve deeper into your emotions and thoughts, exploring the complexity of your experiences.

- Ask yourself probing questions, such as:

- "What emotions surface as I reflect on these experiences?"

- "How have these experiences influenced my beliefs about myself and others?"

- "What patterns or behaviors do I notice in my relationships that may be linked to past trauma?"

4. Finding Strength and Healing:

- As you continue to write, focus on identifying moments of resilience and strength within yourself.

- Explore the ways in which you have coped with and survived emotional abuse, as well as any steps you have taken toward healing.

- Consider what self-care practices or support systems have been helpful to you in reclaiming your sense of self-worth and rebuilding your life.

5. Closing Reflection:

- Take a moment to reflect on your writing journey and the insights you have gained.

- Acknowledge the courage it takes to confront painful experiences and the power of self-expression in the healing process.

- Express gratitude to yourself for engaging in this important act of self-reflection and self-care.

6. Continuing the Journey:

- Commit to regular moments of self-reflection and writing as part of your healing journey.

- Consider seeking additional support from a therapist, counselor, or support group if you feel overwhelmed or in need of guidance.

- Remember that healing is a gradual process, and it's okay to take things one step at a time.

This activity offers you a private and introspective space to explore your experiences of emotional abuse and begin the journey toward healing and self-empowerment through writing. Take your time, be gentle with yourself, and trust in your ability to navigate this journey of self-discovery and growth.

Reflective Questions:

1. Think about times when you felt hurt or controlled in relationships, similar to what was described in the chapter. How did those experiences make you feel, and how do they affect you now?

2. Look at your relationships for any repeating behaviors like manipulation or disrespect. Do you see any patterns that remind you of emotional abuse? How does this change how you see your relationships?

3. Consider what has helped you feel better after tough times. What things do you do to take care of yourself? How do you plan to keep doing those things or find new ways to feel better?

4. Think about times you felt strong, even when things were hard. What helped you get through those tough times? How do those moments make you feel about yourself?

5. Focus on being kind to yourself, especially when thinking about difficult things. How can you be nicer to yourself when you're remembering tough times? What can you say to yourself to feel better?

Take your time with each prompt, allowing yourself to delve deep into your thoughts and emotions. Remember, this is your journey of self-discovery and healing, and you deserve the time and space to explore it fully.

"

You were given this life because you are strong enough to live it.

,,

- Unknown

Chapter 2

BREAKING FREE FROM THE CHAINS OF ABUSE

Abuse, in every form, is a terrible thing that deeply hurts people and causes a lot of pain. It's like a dark cloud that overshadows even the happiest days. In this chapter, I want to make it clear that abuse is never okay, and those caught in such situations should find the strength to get away. I use my own story to show how important it is to recognize and escape from abusive relationships.

"Why me?" is a question that often troubles those stuck in abusive situations. But maybe a better question is, "Why not me?" The Bible says in Jeremiah 1:5, "Before I formed thee in the belly I knew thee, and before thou camest forth out of the womb I sanctified thee, and I ordained thee a prophet unto the nations."

I was just nine years old, around the time I began menstruating. I remember feeling scared and confused, and my mom was in a state of shock. Things were pretty good when I was younger, with caring parents, a hardworking dad, and a mom who stayed at home.

But as I got older and started going through puberty, I began to feel things that I just couldn't talk to my mom about.

Soon after, my parents' marriage hit a rough patch. My mother started a relationship with a man, which resulted in her getting pregnant. This led my father to file for divorce. The divorce proceedings took a dramatic turn when custody was awarded to my father, and my mother lost not only her belongings but also her children. My two younger sisters were present at the trial. At that time, my brothers and I were in Benton, MS, staying with relatives. Watching our parents' marriage fall apart was incredibly hard, and the judge's decision began a very difficult time for us.

The emotional turmoil that followed was devastating. Driven by desperation, my mother did something unthinkable: she shot my father. We heard about this shocking incident back in Benton, and it filled me with fear and confusion. My father survived but was critically injured, while my mother was arrested and faced the possibility of a long prison sentence. She ended up serving 8 years, during which I was separated from my parents and left in the care of other relatives.

As my father slowly got better, my siblings and I were passed around among various family members who gave us a place to stay during that tough time. Their kindness and generosity were like a light in the darkness. I'm especially thankful to my aunt and her husband, who welcomed us into their home with open arms and supported us through everything.

Although my father had recovered and returned home to be with his kids, I had already started down a path of rebellion and defiance that led me into a dangerous situation. I fell for a guy who at first seemed charming and attractive, but he soon turned out to be dark and controlling. His abuse, both hitting and yelling, became a constant nightmare, and I started to regret running away to be with him. Despite the growing tension and my father's attempts to find me, I stubbornly stayed with my boyfriend.

The abuse left deep emotional scars and made me feel worthless. It was only with the help of a friend who saw how bad things were that I managed to break free from the toxic relationship. Going back home meant dealing with the chaos and pain that had spread within my family. The abuse was both physical and emotional, with the emotional part often being deeper and lasting longer.

In the next few pages, we will look at the journey of healing from the deep psychological effects of abuse, losing one's sense of self, and the breakdown of self-worth and values. Abuse often messes up healthy emotional connections and makes it hard to trust others. As I came out from under the shadow of my abusive relationship, I found it hard to trust anyone. It felt like I was looking through a broken lens, always doubting the motives of people around me.

Once, a friend reached out, offering a helping hand and a kind word. I hesitated to accept it because I was caught in a web of skepticism. Was their kindness real, or just another act? Having been shaped by abuse, I was always on guard. But eventually, I took a chance and accepted their support. Over time, this friendship turned into a source of hope, showing me that trust could be rebuilt and relationships fixed.

The mental scars from abuse can lead to serious mental health issues like anxiety, depression, and post-traumatic stress disorder. The impact doesn't just hurt your heart—it digs deep into your mind. Anxiety became a constant presence in my life, trapping me in a relentless cycle of fear and worry. The world seemed like a dangerous place, and I was always tense, even without any clear danger.

Then, there were the days when depression took over. I'd sit alone in my room, looking out at a colorless world. Happiness felt like a thing of the past, and even getting out of bed seemed too hard. But with counseling and strong support from friends and family, I began to see the world's beauty again.

Emotional pain is a common struggle for those who've faced abuse, showing up in many different ways. There were times when guilt and shame weighed heavily on me, leading to bursts of anger and deep sadness, even though those feelings were misplaced.

I remember one time when I was in a room full of friends laughing and telling stories. Out of nowhere, a painful memory from my abusive past came back—I was being hit repeatedly by my ex-boyfriend. Tears started to flow, and I had to leave the room, overwhelmed by my emotions. It was a stark reminder of how deep emotional wounds can go. But by sharing these tough moments, even when it feels uncomfortable, we can start healing and connect with others who've gone through similar experiences.

Abuse can make you lose yourself, clouding your identity and making you feel like just a shadow of who you are. But remember, you're not alone. You have inner strength and resilience that can help you get through the toughest times.

Activity

Healing Exercise: Empowering Self-Rediscovery

Healing from the psychological damage caused by abuse, rediscovering your identity, and rebuilding self-worth and values is a deeply personal journey towards regaining your strength and sense of self. Here's a helpful exercise and five reflective questions to guide you through this healing process:

Materials Needed:

- Journal or paper

- Pen

- Quiet, comfortable space

Steps:

1. Safe Space Creation:

Find a quiet and comfortable space where you won't be disturbed. Light a candle, burn incense, or play calming music—anything that helps you create a sense of safety and peace.

2. Breathing Exercise:

Close your eyes and take several deep breaths. Inhale slowly for a count of four, hold for four, and exhale for a count of four. Repeat this for a few minutes until you feel centered and grounded.

3. Writing Your Truth:

Open your journal or paper. Begin by writing down how the abuse, loss of identity, and erosion of self-worth have affected you.

Be honest and raw in your descriptions. This is a safe space for you to express your deepest feelings without judgment.

4. Affirmations of Self-Worth:

Next, create a list of affirmations that counteract the negative beliefs you've internalized. For example:

- "I am worthy of love and respect."

- "I deserve to be treated with kindness."

- "I am rebuilding my identity with strength and purpose."

Write these affirmations down and repeat them aloud or in your mind. Let them sink into your consciousness.

5. Visualizing Your Ideal Self:

Close your eyes and envision the person you want to become. Picture yourself whole, healed, and radiating with confidence. What does this person look like? How do they carry themselves? What values do they embody? Take time to immerse yourself in this visualization.

6. Reconnecting with Values:

Reflect on the values that are truly important to you. Write down three core values that you want to guide your life moving forward. These could be things like honesty, compassion, courage, etc.

7. Action Steps:

Finally, jot down three small, achievable actions you can take to honor these values and start rebuilding your sense of self. These could be simple acts of self-care, setting boundaries with others, seeking therapy, or pursuing a hobby you love.

8. Gratitude:

End this exercise by writing down three things you are grateful for in your life right now. Cultivating gratitude can help shift your focus towards the positive aspects of your journey.

Reflective Questions:

1. What emotions are surfacing as I think about my past experiences of abuse and loss of identity? How do these emotions manifest in my body?

2. What beliefs about myself have I adopted as a result of these experiences? Are these beliefs serving me or holding me back?

3. In what ways have I already shown resilience and strength in the face of adversity?

4. What does "regaining my power" look like to me? How will I recognize it when I start to feel empowered?

5. What kind of support do I need on this healing journey? Who can I reach out to for help, guidance, or simply a listening ear?

Remember, healing is a process, and it's okay to take it one step at a time. Be gentle with yourself throughout this journey, and know that you have the strength within you to reclaim your power and rebuild a sense of self-worth and identity.

"

Courage is the power to let go of the familiar.

"

- Raymond Lindquist

Chapter 3

CRUEL REVELATION

Unmasking the Deceitful Charm

Have you ever been swept off your feet by someone who seemed like the perfect Prince Charming? At thirteen and a half, I was completely enchanted by a guy who seemed to say and do all the right things, making me feel like I was living in a fairytale. However, I soon learned that not all fairytales end happily—some characters are more like wolves in sheep's clothing.

One day, while running an errand for my dad at Walmart—his favorite place—I was navigating through the aisles when a stranger came up to me. He introduced himself and asked for my name. I hesitantly told him, and he complimented it. Then he asked if I was seeing anyone. I said no and, mindful of my strict father's rules, asked for his number instead of giving mine. I waited a day before calling him.

When I finally gathered the courage to call, my heart pounded as I heard the phone ring. He picked up on the fourth ring with a friendly hello. We chatted easily, and his humor relaxed me; I was already looking forward to seeing him again.

The chance came when a friend asked me to go out with her, and her sister drove us. This was my opportunity to meet the guy again, so I asked my dad if I could go. With his permission, I was thrilled but had to be sneaky about getting ready. I dressed up quietly, gave my dad a peck on the cheek, and told him I'd be back later. As I left the house, I couldn't stop thinking about the guy and our planned meeting.

I got into the car, excited to see him. We arrived at his house, and he greeted me with a big hug. Since he was older and could drive, he suggested we go for a drive. The music was playing, he held my hand, and I felt a special connection.

We made a quick stop at his cousin's house. Surprisingly, I ran into my cousin there, who was dating his cousin. It's a small world! We said hi and chatted for a bit, but our visit was short. We soon headed to a nearby park to talk and hang out.

We really clicked, and despite my dad's rules about when to be home, he didn't want me to leave. He promised we'd meet again. With a heavy heart, I left, and he made sure I got safely to my cousin's house. I spent that night thinking about him.

The next time we met, things seemed even better. We went back to his cousin's place, and it felt perfect—until I overheard something awful. In a bedroom, he and his cousin were talking about plans to come on to me. I was shocked and didn't know what to do, so I kept quiet.

Later, at the park, he made a move to get more physical. I felt pressured and unsure but ended up not stopping him. I didn't tell him what I had overheard. After that, I started to see he might just be a smooth talker who says whatever he needs to get what he wants. I started doubting myself and wondered if I made the right choice.

When I got home, I tried calling him to talk about us, but he didn't answer. Days went by, and I couldn't reach him. It turned out he had ghosted me, leaving me feeling used and heartbroken.

Then, out of nowhere, my cousin Jane called with shocking news about the guy I had fallen for. She told me he was a drug dealer with a girlfriend of three years. Jane also shared a terrifying story about him kidnapping and raping her at gunpoint at the same park he used to take me. Hearing her sad voice, I realized how wrong I had been about him.

Hearing Jane's words left me stunned. She told me that John had recently died from AIDS, which happened just a month after I last saw him. She also shared more about his dark and violent side, which really shook me up.

After listening to Jane's awful experiences and thinking about what I went through, I realized that none of this was her fault. It showed that sometimes people can hide their true selves behind a nice front. I suggested that we both get tested for HIV and thankfully, we were both negative.

This experience was a tough lesson, but it taught me to be more careful about who I trust. In the end, I feel like it was God's love that kept me safe, helping me make good choices even when faced with lies and danger.

This chapter of my life opened my eyes. It taught me that things aren't always as they seem and it's important to listen to my gut. Hard times show us how strong we are, and dealing with lies teaches us how to stand up for ourselves.

Realizing the truth behind his charm taught me that deceit is just lying dressed up to look like the truth, and falling for it can hurt us deeply. It can make us doubt others, feel bad about ourselves, and feel deeply betrayed. Finding out who he really was felt like a rude awakening. It was as if the world we had built crumbled, leaving me to deal with a lot of mistrust.

Trust issues often arise from being deceived. It's hard to trust others when someone we believed was honest turns out to be dishonest. I learned that trust needs to be earned, not just given away without thought. It's crucial to be careful and thoughtful in relationships, taking the time to really know someone before letting them close.

Feelings of unworthiness can also stem from deceit. When we find out someone we cared about has lied to us, it's natural to start questioning our own value. We might wonder why we were susceptible to such deceit. It's important to remember that being deceived reflects on the deceiver's character, not our own value. Building self-love and self-esteem is key to healing and moving forward.

Deceit can also lead to feelings of betrayal. Realizing someone we trusted had hidden motives can break the foundation of a relationship. Healing from this betrayal takes time, but it is possible. An important part of healing is forgiving ourselves for any decisions or actions we made under the deception. It's not our fault; we were manipulated.

To heal from the scars of deceit, we need to treat ourselves kindly. We must recognize our feelings, whether it's anger, sadness, or confusion, and give ourselves permission to work through them. Getting support from friends, family, or a therapist can be very helpful in dealing with the emotional aftermath of deceit.

Rebuilding trust, both in ourselves and in others, is also crucial and should be a gradual process. Learning to trust again means setting healthy boundaries and being open to new, honest relationships while still being cautious.

In the end, being deceived taught me a valuable lesson about the importance of being discerning and understanding my own worth. Although the experience was painful, it helped me grow, reminding me that with time and resilience, we can overcome even the toughest deceptions.

Activity

Healing Exercise: Rebuilding Trust Within Yourself

Healing from betrayal, especially from someone you love and trust, can be a challenging journey. Here is a healing exercise along with five reflective questions to help regain a feeling of trust in your ability to discern:

Materials Needed:

- Journal or paper

- Pen

- Quiet, comfortable space

Steps:

1. Safe and Calm Environment:

Find a quiet, comfortable space where you feel safe. This could be a corner of your home, a park, or anywhere you won't be disturbed.

2. Grounding Exercise:

Close your eyes and take several deep breaths. Feel your feet on the ground or your body supported by a chair. Focus on the sensation of your breath entering and leaving your body. This helps to bring your awareness to the present moment.

3. Journaling Your Feelings:

Open your journal or paper and begin by writing about the betrayal you experienced. Describe how it made you feel, what thoughts arose, and the impact it has had on your ability to trust yourself and others.

4. Identifying Triggers:

Reflect on any triggers or situations that make you feel especially vulnerable or anxious since the betrayal. Write these down, as recognizing them is the first step to managing them.

5. Exploring Your Intuition:

Recall a time when you trusted your intuition, and it served you well. Write about this experience in detail—what led you to trust your gut, how it felt, and the positive outcome. This helps reconnect you with your innate ability to discern.

6. Affirmations of Self-Trust:

Create a list of affirmations that focus on trusting yourself and your instincts. For example:

- "I trust my intuition to guide me."

- "I am capable of making wise decisions."

- "I listen to my inner voice with confidence."

Write these affirmations down and repeat them to yourself daily.

7. Visualizing Trust:

Close your eyes and visualize yourself surrounded by a sphere of glowing light. This light represents trust and wisdom. Imagine it filling you with a sense of security and clarity. Spend a few moments in this visualization, absorbing its positive energy.

8. Setting Boundaries:

Reflect on what boundaries you need to set to protect yourself moving forward. Write down three boundaries that are important for you to establish in relationships to feel safe and respected.

9. Action Steps:

Think of three small actions you can take to honor your intuition and rebuild trust within yourself. These could be things like journaling daily, practicing mindfulness, or seeking therapy.

Reflective Questions:

1. How has the betrayal impacted my ability to trust myself and others?

2. What warning signs or red flags did I ignore or dismiss before the betrayal occurred? How can I learn from these signs moving forward?

3. What does trusting myself and my intuition feel like? Can I recall a time when I trusted myself, and it turned out well?

4. In what ways can I nurture and honor my intuition in my daily life?

5. What are the qualities and behaviors I now seek in others to establish trust? How can I communicate my boundaries effectively?

Remember, healing takes time and patience. Be gentle with yourself as you navigate this process of rebuilding trust within yourself. Trust is a journey, and by reconnecting with your intuition and setting healthy boundaries, you can regain a sense of confidence in your ability to discern and trust again.

"

The truth will set you free, but first, it will piss you off.

"

- Gloria Steinem

Chapter 4

SHATTERED TRUST

Broken But Survived

At fourteen, I joined a dating site and met Joseph, a nineteen-year-old cook at the Waffle House. One Friday night, I asked my cousin Bonita to drive me to his house. Upon arriving, I hesitated, but Bonita encouraged me, reminding me that I was already there and it might be worth giving it a shot. Despite still feeling wary from past hurts, I decided to take a chance on Joseph, who seemed different.

When we got there, Joseph came out to greet us. He struck up a conversation about his aspirations and life goals, which helped me lower my guard slightly. Over time, as I got to know him better, I felt safe and connected with him deeply. In a moment of impulsiveness, driven by our connection, I got his name tattooed on my body after we discussed getting matching tattoos. However, when I asked when he would get mine, he refused, citing money problems and denying he ever agreed to our plan.

His refusal shattered me, leaving me feeling guilty for moving too quickly and trusting he would reciprocate. It was a harsh lesson, but instead of walking away, I stayed, curious to see how things would evolve. One evening, while we were in his car, his phone kept ringing, and he ignored it, which raised my suspicions. The following day, there was a noticeable shift in his mood, and despite my attempts to cheer him up, he remained downcast. We gradually spent less time together, and communication dwindled. I couldn't shake the feeling that something was wrong.

Driven by concern and regret, I visited his duplex, only to find his and another car in the driveway. My heart sank. I knocked, but he didn't answer. I left feeling more alone than ever, realizing I might never understand why I gave him a chance in the first place.

I was swamped with feelings of rejection, confusion, and hurt. It seemed that he had been avoiding me, and I couldn't understand why. Following that ordeal, I slipped into a depression. The burden of heartbreak was heavy, leading to a loss of interest in things I once loved, reduced appetite, and constant flashbacks to those painful memories. I withdrew from my friends and isolated myself.

Depression is a tough battle, but slowly, over a month, I began to find myself again. I didn't go to church much as a young adult, but my grandmother took me when I was a kid. Reflecting on those times, I remembered a scripture from Isaiah 61:3 that says, "To appoint unto them that mourn in Zion, to give unto them beauty for ashes, the oil of joy for mourning, the garment of praise for the spirit of heaviness." This verse reminded me that transformation is possible after loss.

Heartbreak truly breaks your spirit and leaves you searching for who you are. Through self-reflection and digging deep, you start to find your worth, understand your weaknesses and strengths, and redefine your path. Heartbreak brings sadness, hurt, and a lot of overthinking and trying to make sense of things.

To heal and cope, it's important to accept your feelings, talk to someone you trust, and get professional help if it gets too overwhelming. Getting back into your hobbies and interests can help bring back your excitement for life. Time, self-care, and support are key to healing from heartbreak, allowing you eventually to step out of the shadows into a stronger version of yourself. I battled self-doubt and blamed myself for what happened. It was a dark and challenging time, but as time went on, I began to heal.

Through self-discovery, I learned the value of self-worth and setting healthy boundaries in relationships. I discovered that trust needs to be earned, and rushing into relationships can lead to regrets.

With time, I found my way out of the darkness. I learned that heartbreak, though painful, isn't the end but a chance to grow. The experience made me more cautious in relationships. It taught me to value myself more and lean on loved ones in tough times.

Heartbreak may break the spirit, but it also can lead to growth and self-discovery. I came out of this phase with a deeper understanding of who I am and what I deserve in a relationship. Though the scars of deceit and betrayal remain, they remind me of the strength and resilience I have. While initially shattered by the betrayal and deceit I faced, I ultimately emerged from this ordeal stronger and wiser.

Activity

Healing Exercise: Cultivating Self-Compassion

Experiencing depression caused by rejection can be a deeply challenging and painful experience. Here is a healing exercise along with five reflective questions that can assist in navigating this difficult time:

Materials Needed:

- Journal or paper

- Pen

- Comfortable, quiet space

Steps:

1. Create a Safe Space:

Find a quiet and comfortable place where you can sit without interruptions. Light a candle or some incense if it helps create a sense of peace.

2. Breathing Exercise:

Close your eyes and take slow, deep breaths. Inhale deeply through your nose, hold for a moment, and then exhale fully through your mouth. Repeat this several times, focusing on the rhythm of your breath.

3. Writing Your Feelings:

Open your journal or paper. Begin by writing down all the feelings you are experiencing due to the rejection. Allow yourself to be completely honest and open. Write about the pain, sadness, anger, or any other emotions that come up.

4. Letter of Release:

Write a letter to the person who rejected you. This letter is not to be sent to anyone; it is for your own healing. Express your feelings without holding back. You can write about how their rejection has affected you, what you wish they knew, and anything else you need to get off your chest.

5. Self-Compassion Affirmations:

Create a list of self-compassionate affirmations. These can be phrases like:

- "I am deserving of love and respect."

- "I acknowledge my pain, and it is okay to feel this way."

- "I am resilient, and I will get through this "

Write these affirmations down and repeat them to yourself, either silently or out loud.

6. Identifying Support:

Reflect on who in your life can provide support during this time. Write down the names of friends, family members, or professionals you can reach out to for help and understanding.

7. Gratitude Journaling:

Shift your focus towards gratitude by writing down three things you are grateful for today, no matter how small. This practice can help bring a sense of positivity amidst the pain.

8. Visualization:

Close your eyes and visualize a warm, comforting light surrounding you. Imagine this light as a symbol of healing and self-love. See it filling you with warmth and reassurance, soothing the pain of rejection.

Reflective Questions:

1. What specific thoughts or beliefs about myself are triggered by this rejection? Are these beliefs based on reality, or are they distorted by the pain of the experience?

2. In what ways can I show myself compassion and kindness during this challenging time? What self-care practices can I incorporate into my daily routine?

3. How has this rejection highlighted areas of growth or self-discovery for me? What lessons can I take away from this experience?

4. What kind of relationship do I want to have with myself moving forward? How can I cultivate self-love and acceptance, regardless of external validation?

5. What are some positive aspects of my life that I can focus on right now? How can I shift my attention towards these sources of joy and fulfillment?

Remember, healing from rejection and depression takes time and patience. Allow yourself to feel the emotions fully, and know that it is okay to seek professional help if needed. You are not alone, and there is hope for brighter days ahead.

"

Strength doesn't come from what you can do. It comes from overcoming the things you once thought you couldn't.

"

- Rikki Rogers

Chapter 5

SCARS OF LOVE

A Journey Through Turmoil and Finding Light in Darkness

In 1996, my life changed dramatically when I started dating a guy named Frank. We were both in high school and really into each other, treasuring every chance we got to be together. We couldn't wait for school to end each day so we could see each other. However, one day would forever alter my life.

That day, Frank and I decided to skip school with a little help from my cousin Gina, who was dating Frank's brother Timothy. She picked us up, and we ended up at Frank's brother's house. Looking back, it feels like everything that day led us to that bedroom. Young and naive, we didn't think things through the way we would have later on. What happened next was a story of young people making hasty decisions based more on feelings than clear thinking.

As the hours passed in that bedroom, one thing led to another, and we got intimate. Strangely, I did not regret it, and, surprisingly, Frank did not abandon me afterward as so many young men might in a similar situation. Our lives quickly became more connected than we could have imagined when I found out I was pregnant just a month later. Frank was thrilled about the news, but my dad was really upset. I also went through a tough time with morning sickness; it was so intense that there were days I just couldn't make it to school.

Once the morning sickness passed, I started to feel a deep sense of shame as my belly grew. The bigger I got, the heavier the shame weighed on me. Eventually, it became too much, and at just fifteen, I made the tough decision to drop out of school, realizing I couldn't keep up with my studies while preparing to become a mom.

Becoming a mother was a rocky journey right from the start. When it was time for my son to be born, his dad wasn't there in the delivery room. Instead, my dad and my Aunt Linda were there to support me. It didn't take long for him to hear about his son and start visiting, although my dad didn't fully approve and only allowed short visits.

One day, my son's father asked me a question that would change everything: "Would you like to move in with me at my mom's house?" I didn't hesitate to say yes, driven by my feelings for Frank and my desire for our child to have something like a family. I left my dad's house, fully aware of his disappointment, and started a new chapter by moving into Frank's mom, Pam's, house. The transition was awkward as I tried to figure out how to live with Frank and his mom under the same roof.

For a short time, living at Pam's house seemed to bring some stability. But soon, problems between Frank and his mother came up. Pam urged him to take more responsibility now that he was a dad, making our already difficult situation even more complex. Frank decided to leave his mom's house during one argument, plunging our young family into uncertainty.

Frank took me to an abandoned house, where we stayed for a few days. As things got worse, we ended up in a motel, which was far from ideal. The area was known for drug use and crime, and one night, our room was suddenly pounded on by the police. They were raiding the place for drug activities. We weren't arrested, but we were harshly told to leave and never return. Realizing we needed a safer place for our child, I looked to Frank for a plan.

Reluctantly, we moved back to his mother's house. Pam let us come back mainly because she was worried about her grandchild. But soon, a darker side of Frank emerged. He became controlling and abusive, dictating what I could do and where I could go. Our arguments often turned into verbal and physical fights. One Saturday morning, things escalated in the kitchen, and Frank punched the wall next to me. A picture frame hit me, cutting my eyelid and leaving me bleeding and in tears. Despite knowing I didn't deserve this treatment, my feelings for Frank made it hard to leave.

The hardest part of this journey was feeling stuck in this abusive relationship because of my love for him. It became even clearer that he didn't feel the same when he started seeing another woman named Keisha. One Saturday afternoon, he brought Keisha home and told me she was five months pregnant with his child, just as I was five months pregnant with our second. His actions were not only heartbreaking but also showed a deep disrespect towards me.

To make the situation even more unbearable, Frank started bringing Keisha into his mother's house while I was still living there. It was ridiculous and painful and served as a harsh lesson that people will treat you as badly as you let them. Despite the infidelity and humiliation, I didn't take any decisive steps to leave. As a result, I ended up with a sexually transmitted disease that I didn't even know I had.

One day, representatives from a sexually transmitted disease clinic showed up at Frank's mother's house. I found myself in the back of a van, headed to a place I never imagined I'd visit. It was a humiliating and deeply embarrassing experience. At the clinic, I faced a barrage of questions and medical tests.

The diagnosis was devastating: I had contracted gonorrhea. The treatment was painful, involving a shot and a course of penicillin pills. This ordeal left deep physical and emotional scars, making me feel like damaged goods, tainted by a past I couldn't escape. This should have been enough reason to leave Frank, but I stayed, clinging to a faint hope that he would change.

When Frank came home late that night, I confronted him about the disease. But he refused to take responsibility or acknowledge his role in what happened. All he could say was, "I want our relationship to work. I don't want to lose you." Naive and gullible, I believed him and decided to give him another chance, not realizing the gravity of the situation. Trust has to be earned, and I failed to see that Frank was not deserving of mine.

Two weeks later, my condition worsened significantly. I became incredibly weak, unable to stand or eat. Late one night, my condition deteriorated so much that I had to be rushed to the hospital. Upon arrival, the medical staff hurried to assist me. I was so ill, lying on a hospital bed, when the doctor told me to count backward from ten as they placed an oxygen mask over my face. I don't remember anything after that. I woke up in the recovery room, and the doctor came to explain why I was there.

His words crushed me. He said, "Ms. Lee, do you know why you are here? You were brought in last night because your appendix was about to rupture, and if you hadn't been brought here when you were, you might not have survived." Tears filled my eyes as I lay there, taking in the gravity of what I had just been through and the additional stress that my relationship had placed on my health.

The doctor informed me that I had chlamydia, which had severely impacted my health, almost causing my appendix to rupture. He also mentioned that the damage was so extensive that it might be impossible for me to have more children. In that moment, I felt overwhelmed with shame and guilt for trusting Frank. However, I held onto my faith, believing that God had the final say despite what the doctor predicted. Despite the dire prognosis, I went on to have four more children, defying the doctor's expectations.

During this difficult period, my cousin Ghameka, who was like a sister to me, learned about my struggles. She reached out and promised to help me escape from the toxic environment I was in. True to her word, the following week, she came and took me away. I left with her and never looked back. I often say she was my guardian angel because I didn't have the strength or courage to leave on my own. It felt like the enemy was trying to take my life, but God wasn't ready for me yet. I still had a purpose to fulfill for Him.

This experience underscored the unpredictable nature of life, filled with challenges and moments of deep despair. Yet, through it all, I remained determined to find a way out. I refused to let the scars of my past dictate my future because I believed that God had a plan to transform them into a source of strength and resilience.

If you are facing a tough situation, battling personal demons, or dealing with the consequences of past mistakes, I want to share a message of hope and resilience. Remember, you are not alone in your struggles. Everyone has their battles, mistakes, and moments of despair. Knowing that others have faced similar challenges and come out stronger can offer comfort and motivation.

Believe in the power of time. There's a saying, "Time heals all wounds." It might seem like the pain will last forever, but with each day, you're moving away from the toughest times. Time gives you a chance to think things over, grow, and see your life from a new angle.

Reach out for support and connection. Don't hesitate to lean on friends or family or get professional help. Talking to someone you trust can really help, and they can guide you or just listen. Remember, it's okay to be open and vulnerable.

Understand that the scars you have can turn into your strengths. Every challenge you've gone through and every scar you have shows how strong you are. These experiences mold you and prepare you to handle future challenges with more bravery and wisdom.

Most importantly, believe in a bigger plan. Whether your faith is in God, the universe, or just the idea that there's a reason for everything, know that these tough times can be steps to something better. Just like I believed that my struggles would strengthen me, you can keep the faith that your pain has a purpose.

To wrap it up, life might take us through some really tough spots, but those are the times we find out how strong we really are. Whether it's God, the universe, or just how things turn out, there might be a plan to turn your hard times into strengths. So, keep up the hope. Accept your past as part of your story, knowing it can lead you to better days. Hold onto your strength, seek help when needed, and remember, you can rise from the darkness into a new, brighter day.

Activity

Healing Exercise: Releasing Hurt and Rebuilding Self-Worth

Experiencing hurt from infidelity and shame can be incredibly challenging and painful. Here is a healing exercise along with five reflective questions to assist in this difficult process:

Materials Needed:

- Journal or paper

- Pen

- Comfortable, quiet space

Steps:

1. Safe Space Creation:

Find a quiet and comfortable space where you won't be disturbed. Create a calming atmosphere with soft lighting, candles, or soothing music. Take a few deep breaths to center yourself.

2. Writing Your Truth:

Open your journal or paper. Begin by writing down all the emotions and thoughts you are experiencing related to infidelity and shame. Let yourself express the hurt, anger, sadness, and any other feelings without holding back.

3. Letter Writing:

Write a letter to the person who caused the hurt. You don't have to send this letter; it's for your healing process. Express how their actions have affected you, how you feel betrayed and hurt, and how it has impacted your sense of self-worth. Be honest and raw in your words.

4. Self-Compassion Exercise:

Write a letter to yourself from a place of deep self-compassion and understanding. Acknowledge the pain you are feeling and offer yourself kindness and forgiveness. Remind yourself that you are worthy of love and respect, regardless of what has happened.

5. Release Ritual:

Tear up or burn the letter to the person who caused the hurt, symbolizing your release of the pain and betrayal. As you do this, visualize letting go of the negative emotions and making space for healing and self-love.

6. Affirmations of Self-Worth:

Create a list of affirmations that uplift and empower you. Some examples include:

- "I deserve to be treated with love and respect."
- "I release shame and embrace my worthiness."
- "I am healing and growing stronger every day."

Repeat these affirmations daily, either aloud or in your mind.

7. Reconnecting with Self:

Take some time to engage in activities that bring you joy and peace. This could be going for a walk in nature, listening to uplifting music, practicing yoga or meditation, or spending time with supportive friends or family members.

Reflective Questions:

1. What are the core beliefs about myself that have been shaken by this experience of infidelity and shame? How do these beliefs impact my self-worth?

2. How can I show myself compassion and forgiveness for what has happened? How can I practice self-care during this difficult time?

3. What boundaries do I need to set for myself moving forward to protect my heart and well-being? How can I communicate these boundaries effectively?

4. What lessons can I take from this experience that can help me grow and become more resilient? How can I turn this pain into an opportunity for personal development?

5. Who are the people in my life I can trust and lean on for support? How can I open up to them about what I'm going through?

Remember that healing is a journey, and seeking professional support is okay if needed. Be patient and gentle with yourself as you navigate through this process of healing and rebuilding your self-worth.

"

Out of difficulties grow miracles.

"

- Jean de La Bruyère

Chapter 6

ALMOST LOST MY MIND

In 2001, I met a guy named Ricky at Barry's convenience store in Benton, Mississippi. He was twenty-six, and I was twenty. He grabbed my attention with his smart and charming ways. We hit it off right away, swapping phone numbers, and I was excited about this new connection. Little did I know that this promising start would lead to a rough path of manipulation and abuse.

Our first dates were full of laughs and shared dreams. Ricky was all charm, and I fell hard for his charismatic ways. We decided to make it official, and I couldn't have been happier. But things took a sharp turn when I got pregnant in 2001, and our daughter was born in 2002.

As we settled into parenthood, Ricky began to change. He would disappear for days, leaving me and our newborn to fend for ourselves. This cycle of him leaving was emotionally crushing. I felt alone, overwhelmed and unsure about what to do. Eventually, I hit my limit and decided to leave Ricky.

I called my Aunt Linda and her husband Vernon, who helped me move out. It was tough, but I couldn't take Ricky's unpredictable ways anymore. However, my feelings for him muddled my thinking. When he came back apologizing and promising to change, I took him back. We got back together, but it wasn't long before the abuse started.

One day, things boiled over, and we had a massive fight that turned physical. Ricky attacked me, leaving me scared and shaken. After he let me go, I ran to his mom, Patricia, and told her everything. She made him leave the house, but I was still stuck in this harmful cycle of forgiving him and hoping for better.

A month later, I found out I was pregnant again. Despite everything, I wanted to believe Ricky would change. We moved into a new apartment, hoping for a fresh start, but it was clear Ricky hadn't changed at all. He was just waiting for a chance to start manipulating and controlling me again.

One Saturday, Ricky's brother, Steve, came over. That visit was a turning point. Ricky started treating me badly, putting me down and humiliating me in front of Steve. The situation got worse, and Ricky attacked me again, causing serious injuries. Steve ended up calling an ambulance, and as I lay there unable to move, Ricky walked out.

I gave birth prematurely to our second daughter, who weighed just one pound, after a traumatic fall during an argument. Ricky's absence during this tough time made my pain and resentment even deeper. My baby spent a month in the ICU, and Ricky didn't visit her even once. When she was finally able to come home from the hospital, I had to face the harsh truth about our situation.

Ricky returned in January 2003, full of apologies and saying he had changed. He asked for forgiveness, promising to be there for our daughter. Even though I had my doubts, I thought about giving him another chance, mostly because I was scared of raising our kids alone. Looking back, I realize that fear was driving my decisions, making me stay in a bad relationship instead of facing the challenges of being a single parent. Ricky had shown his true colors early on, but I had ignored the signs. After taking him back, things were okay for a while until one Saturday afternoon when some friends and family came over. They were all hanging out under a tree, laughing and having a good time. I walked outside to ask him something.

I was wearing a simple outfit, a two-piece shorts set, which wasn't revealing at all, but I saw anger and madness in his eyes. He stood up, rushed over, grabbed my arm, and started yelling in my face, accusing me of trying to show off my body to the guys there. No matter how much I tried to explain, he wouldn't listen. Suddenly, he took off his shirt, threw it on the ground, clenched his fist, and punched me in the mouth, leaving me with a swollen lip. When his mother saw what was happening, she rushed outside, confronted him, and made him leave. She insisted that I call a relative who lived nearby to come and get me. She told me I didn't deserve what her son was putting me through, so I left that day.

When someone shows you who they are, believe them. I learned this the hard way. Love shouldn't blind you to the point where you put up with mistreatment. Instead, it should empower you to set boundaries and look out for your own well-being.

Reflecting on my experiences, I now see that choosing to be a single parent over staying in a toxic relationship was the right decision. Staying with Ricky would have meant exposing my children to domestic violence and an unhealthy atmosphere, which was something I couldn't allow. The scars from those hard years will always be with me, but they remind me of the strength and resilience I discovered in myself. While my path was full of manipulation and abuse, it ultimately brought me to a place where I could grow, learn about myself, and work towards a better future for me and my kids.

Looking back, I see that fear influenced many of my choices, pushing me to stay in a bad relationship rather than face the challenges of parenting alone. Let me tell you more about that critical time in my life, which I hope can resonate with you and give you strength in your journey.

I remember feeling incredibly scared as a young mom, unsure if I could handle the responsibilities of parenting by myself. The idea of being a single mom seemed overwhelming, and I kept asking myself: "Can I really do this without him?"

Fear can cloud your judgment. It distorts how you see things and makes you second-guess yourself. I wanted to believe Ricky when he promised he'd change because the thought of facing the world as a single parent terrified me. The idea of handling the responsibilities and uncertainties of raising my kids alone felt like too much to bear.

This fear kept me tied to a relationship that was unhealthy and toxic, where emotional and physical abuse became the norm. It's important to recognize that I wasn't alone in this experience. Many people find themselves stuck in harmful relationships because they're afraid of what lies ahead. The thought of stepping into a new chapter of life, especially with children involved, can feel completely overwhelming.

But here's the deeper truth: fear is a common human emotion. We all feel it at different times, especially when we're about to make big changes or face tough decisions. It's important to remember that fear can protect us, but it can also motivate us.

In my case, fear initially paralyzed me, keeping me in a damaging relationship. But it also pushed me to make a change. It was the fear of letting my children grow up in an abusive environment, the fear of risking their well-being, that finally gave me the strength to break free.

Fear doesn't have to trap us. It can also be the key to our freedom. It can push us to make hard choices that are better for us and our children. Through the darkest times, I found a spark of courage within me, and that courage grew with every tough step I took.

So, my message to you is this: don't be beaten down by your fears. Recognize them, embrace them as part of your journey, and use them to make positive changes in your life. Like me, you might find that your fears can drive you to make the bravest decisions, leading you to a brighter future.

Activity

Healing Exercise: Nurturing Self-Compassion and Safety

Experiencing domestic abuse and abandonment can have deep and lasting effects on a person's mental, emotional, and physical well-being. Here is a healing exercise tailored to address these traumas, along with five reflective questions for each topic:

Materials Needed:

- Journal or paper

- Pen

- Comfortable, safe space

Steps:

1. Creating a Safe Space:

Find a quiet and comfortable place where you feel safe. This could be a corner of your home, a cozy nook, or anywhere you can relax without interruptions. Light a candle, burn incense, or play calming music if it helps you feel at ease.

2. Breathing and Grounding:

Close your eyes and take a few deep breaths. Breathe in deeply through your nose, hold it for a second, and then slowly breathe out through your mouth. As you exhale, picture yourself letting go of any tension and fear. Feel yourself becoming more relaxed and centered in the present moment.

3. Writing Your Truth:

Open your journal or paper. Begin by writing down your experiences of domestic abuse and abandonment. Let yourself express the pain, fear, anger, and any other emotions you're carrying. This is a safe space for you to be completely honest with yourself.

4. Letter Writing - Releasing Resentment:

Write a letter to the person(s) who abused you or abandoned you. You don't need to send this letter; it's for your healing process. Express all the anger, hurt, and resentment you feel towards them. Then, when you're ready, forgive them. This forgiveness is for your own well-being, not to excuse their actions.

5. Nurturing Self-Compassion:

Write a letter to yourself from a place of deep self-compassion and understanding. Acknowledge the pain you've endured and reassure yourself that you are worthy of love and safety. Write down affirmations such as:

- "I deserve to be treated with respect and kindness."

- "I am strong and resilient."

- "I am creating a safe and loving space within myself."

6. Creating a Safety Plan:

If you're still in a situation of abuse or fear, create a safety plan for yourself. Include steps to protect yourself, such as contacting a trusted friend or family member, finding a safe place to stay, or contacting a domestic violence hotline.

7. Symbolic Release:

Find a small object that represents the pain and trauma you're carrying. It could be a stone, a piece of paper, or anything meaningful to you. Take this object outside and release it. You can bury it, throw it into the water, or simply leave it behind. As you do this, visualize releasing the burden and reclaiming your freedom.

Reflective Questions– Domestic Abuse:

1. What were the warning signs of abuse in my past relationship? How can I use this knowledge to recognize and avoid similar situations in the future?

2. How has the abuse impacted my sense of self-worth and self-esteem? In what ways can I begin rebuilding my self-confidence?

3. What resources are available to me for support and protection? How can I reach out for help when I need it?

4. How has the experience of abandonment shaped my beliefs about trust and intimacy? In what ways can I work on trusting myself and others again?

5. In what areas of my life do I feel a sense of loss or emptiness due to abandonment? How can I begin to fill these spaces with self-love and self-care?

Remember that healing is a process, and being patient and gentle with yourself as you navigate these deep wounds is important. Seeking therapy or counseling can also be incredibly beneficial on your journey toward healing and reclaiming your sense of self-worth and safety.

"

*Even the darkest night will end,
and the sun will rise.*

"

- Victor Hugo

Chapter 7

BETRAYAL AND REDEMPTION

A Journey Through Infidelity

There's an old saying my parents often used: "You make your bed hard, you lie in it." I never thought I'd be facing that situation so soon.

Back in 2010, I decided to try online dating and ended up meeting a man who looked like he could be the start of something great. We first connected on a dating site, and after he sent me a message, we got into some really interesting talks that piqued my interest. He was charming, and our conversations were so good that I found myself getting more and more attracted to him. Soon, we were talking every day, and our bond just kept getting stronger.

Meeting him in real life was exciting but also a bit scary. What if he wasn't who he said he was? What if it turned out to be dangerous? But as we kept talking, I felt more confident about meeting him.

He lived in Canton, and I was in Jackson. He invited me over one Saturday, and I decided to go for it.

When the day came, I was nervous but excited. I put a lot of thought into what I wore: black leggings, a stylish black blouse, and sandals with a bit of bling. I added some silver bracelets and earrings to complete the look. Then, I drove my 2006 Brown Chevy Cavalier to Canton.

He gave me a warm hug when I got there. Holding my hand, he led me into his house and told me to make myself at home. He was so kind and polite that I felt comfortable right away, although a tiny part of me was still unsure. But I didn't let that bother me too much.

We ended up having a great evening. We laughed a lot, talked about our kids, and found out we had more in common than we thought. Our connection grew stronger as the night went on. When I left the next day, all I could think about was him and what our future might look like. I pictured a family where our kids were happy and loved.

It only took three months before I felt ready to introduce him to my kids, which was a big deal for our relationship. When I mentioned it to him, he was totally on board. He was 48, quite a bit older than me, but his maturity and understanding only made me value our relationship more. He really seemed like "the one."

Meeting my kids went way better than I expected. He was so warm and generous with them, and in no time, he was bonding with them—giving them gifts and doing all sorts of activities together.

As time went on, our relationship grew stronger, and we also grew closer to God. In 2010, he proposed to me at our church, and by 2012, we were getting married. It was a beautiful day filled with family and friends, and it felt like the perfect start to our life together. Standing at the altar, looking into each other's eyes, and listening to the pastor, I realized the seriousness of the commitment I was making. I had some fears and doubts, but I pushed those aside as we exchanged vows and sealed our commitment with a kiss.

The first days of our married life were blissful and full of promise. But things got tougher when we blended our families, including my stepson and stepdaughter. Merging our families was a big change, but we were committed to making it work. Though it wasn't always easy, I treated my stepchildren as my own. A major challenge came with my stepdaughter's behavior.

She had had a tough time growing up—her aunt had to take care of her while her birth mother was in prison. I tried my best to welcome her into our family, but her actions started to worry me. Once, I caught her lying to her father about me, and I had to step in to set things straight. Unfortunately, my husband didn't handle it as I hoped, leaving me feeling pretty powerless as a stepmom.

The issues with my stepdaughter put a strain on our marriage, causing me and my husband to grow apart as we tried to deal with the changing dynamics at home. It was a tough time that really tested the strength of our family.

During this time of emotional distance between us, I made a decision that had a major impact on our marriage. I sought comfort and affection outside our relationship. I got back in touch with my childhood friend Danny, someone I hadn't spoken to in years. As we caught up, I ended up sharing the troubles I was facing in my marriage. He showed interest in meeting up, and I agreed. One day, I secretly met him after my husband went to work.

We met in a Walmart parking lot, and seeing him there, I felt torn inside. I knew it was wrong, but I went ahead with the meeting anyway. We caught up on old times, and he asked to see me again. I said yes, even though I knew it was betraying my marriage. We met again at the same place, and I couldn't stop myself from going with him to a hotel.

As time went on, I continued to see Danny secretly. We'd meet in that same parking lot, sometimes grabbing a meal or a drink at a restaurant before heading to a hotel. After each meeting, I was overwhelmed with guilt, feeling more conflicted and tormented than ever.

This pattern repeated, and soon, I was back at the hotel again, caught up in the moment with him. The guilt was crushing, overshadowing any brief happiness. When my phone rang and I saw it was my husband, I couldn't answer it. Panicked, I told Danny we had to leave. He drove me back to my car, and as I headed home, I knew I was risking everything important to me.

When I got home, my husband was waiting. He could tell something was off and demanded to know where I had been. I lied and said I was at the store, but he didn't buy it. We ended up having a huge fight, with him accusing me of cheating because of how I'd been acting.

The weight of my secret was crushing me, and I felt like I had to come clean. After he stormed off and sat angrily at the dining table, I knew I couldn't keep hiding what I'd done. After a shower, I went to him, feeling nervous and scared. I finally said, "I need to talk to you. What I'm about to say is really bad, and I hope you can still see me the same way after this."

As tears filled my eyes, I confessed the painful truth, "I cheated, and it was very wrong of me to step outside our marriage. I'm so sorry." My husband's reaction was intense; he started banging his head against the headboard, asking for more details. I admitted it was with Danny and that it had happened twice. I could feel our marriage falling apart.

A month later, my husband moved out, leaving me to care for our eight children alone. With no job and overwhelmed by the responsibility, the guilt of what I did weighed heavily on me. I was forced to confront my mistakes and deal with the consequences by myself.

Two months after he left, my husband came back, hoping to fix things and rebuild our family. But he quickly saw how much damage had been done. While he was gone, out of frustration and stress from managing everything alone, I had thrown away many of his things. Our shaky attempts to make things right didn't last long. One night, when he came to pick up his kids, he left and didn't come back. Now, I was starting a tough journey as a single parent.

The emotional and mental strain that led to my cheating came from unresolved problems in our marriage, feelings of being neglected, loneliness, and a risky curiosity about the past. His actions, like always taking his phone everywhere and hiding messages, made me feel doubtful and insecure. The guilt and shame of my actions haunted me. But I was also struggling with feeling neglected and emotionally cut off in our marriage.

The consequences of my choices hit hard. Splitting from my husband made me feel like I had failed in my marriage, and I was left with a lot of bottled-up guilt that I had to confront directly. I was determined to rebuild my life and create a stable, loving environment for my kids.

Looking back on everything that happened, I realized how crucial communication, trust, and honesty are in a marriage. Ignoring these key elements can slowly wear down even the most promising relationships. My experiences taught me a harsh lesson about the deep impact of cheating and the complex mix of emotions that comes with stepping away from commitments.

This chapter of my life was full of pain, betrayal, remorse, and regret. But it also taught me about personal growth, forgiveness, and the strength of the human spirit. This painful time turned into a critical point in my journey towards self-discovery, taking responsibility, and committing to a better future for me and my kids.

As I tackled the challenges of being a single parent and the tough task of putting my life back together, I knew it wouldn't be easy. However, I was ready to learn from my mistakes, turn my scars into strengths, and find a new sense of purpose. It was time to turn the page and start a new chapter in my life, one filled with growth, healing, and hope for a brighter future.

Activity

Healing Exercise: Acknowledging Betrayal and Seeking Forgiveness

Experiencing the aftermath of betraying a loved one can be an overwhelming and deeply painful journey. If you find yourself grappling with feelings of remorse, regret, and the weight of your actions, know that you are not alone. This healing exercise is designed to guide you through a process of self-reflection, understanding, and ultimately seeking forgiveness.

Materials Needed:

- Journal or paper

- Pen

- Quiet, reflective space

Steps:

1. Creating a Quiet Space:

Find a peaceful and private space where you can reflect without distractions. This could be a corner of your home or a favorite spot outdoors.

2. Deep Breathing:

Sit comfortably and close your eyes. Take several deep breaths, focusing on the inhale and exhale. With each breath, allow yourself to release tension and center your thoughts.

3. Writing Your Truth:

Open your journal or paper. Begin by writing down the specific actions or behaviors that led to the betrayal. Be honest with yourself and acknowledge the impact of your actions on your partner.

4. Exploring Feelings of Remorse and Regret:

Write a letter to your partner expressing your remorse and regret for betraying their trust. Pour out your heart, acknowledging the pain you have caused and the weight of your actions.

5. Identifying Triggers and Patterns:

Reflect on the underlying reasons or triggers that led to the betrayal. Were there unresolved issues or patterns of behavior that contributed to your actions? Write down any insights or realizations.

6. Self-Reflection - Understanding Motivations:

Reflect on your motivations for the betrayal. What were you seeking or trying to avoid? How can you address these needs in healthier ways in the future?

7. Committing to Change:

Write a list of concrete steps you are willing to take to rebuild trust and demonstrate your commitment to change. This could include seeking therapy, attending couples counseling, or making specific changes in your behavior.

8. Seeking Forgiveness - Letter to Your Partner:

Write a letter to your partner asking for their forgiveness. Be sincere and vulnerable in your words, expressing your deep regret and your commitment to earning back their trust. Remember, the purpose of this letter is for your healing process, even if you choose not to send it.

9. Visualizing Reconciliation:

Close your eyes and visualize a positive outcome. Imagine yourself and your partner in a space of healing and reconciliation. Picture trust being rebuilt, communication improving, and the relationship growing stronger.

Reflective Questions:

What specific actions or behaviors led to the betrayal? What emotions or needs were driving these actions?

How has the betrayal impacted your partner? Take time to empathize with their pain and consider the trust that has been broken?

What patterns or triggers contributed to the betrayal? How can you address these underlying issues to prevent similar actions in the future?

In what ways can you demonstrate genuine remorse and commitment to change? Consider concrete steps you can take to rebuild trust and repair the relationship.

What does forgiveness mean to you in this context? How can you work towards earning forgiveness, both from your partner and from yourself?

Remember, healing is a process that requires patience, self-compassion, and a willingness to confront difficult truths. While the journey ahead may be challenging, it is also an opportunity for growth and self-discovery. Seeking support from a therapist or counselor can also be invaluable as you navigate this challenging journey of self-reflection and growth.

"

Sometimes the bad things that happen in our lives put us directly on the path to the best things that will ever happen to us.

"

- Unknown

Chapter 8

THE REBOUND PERSON

Navigating the Pitfalls of Infidelity and Self-Reflection

Galatians 6:7 reminds us, "Be not deceived; God is not mocked: for whatsoever a man soweth, that shall he also reap." These words proved true in my life, teaching me a hard lesson I was about to learn.

After my marriage ended, I entered a relationship with Zack, the man I had an affair with during my marriage. Despite knowing what the Bible says about adultery, such as Matthew's commandment, "Thou shalt not commit adultery," and despite my fear of God, my desires for Zack overpowered my better judgment.

Have you ever been in a relationship for the wrong reasons? I was. It wasn't love that drew me to Zack; it was my fear of facing my vulnerabilities alone. I was still legally married and not yet divorced and being with Zack helped me dodge facing my reality. His attention and affection felt comforting, even though I knew deep down it was wrong.

Life teaches us tough lessons through our mistakes. You'd think I would have learned from my past, but here I was, repeating them. The excitement I felt with Zack was undeniable. Something about his Scorpio traits—his intellect, creativity, romance, and confidence—captivated me. He brought excitement and unpredictability to our relationship.

However, doubts soon began to creep in. I couldn't shake off the feeling that something was off with Zack. Perhaps it was guilt from my own actions. One Tuesday night, he promised a night out, but he never showed up. He ignored my calls and messages, leaving me confused and suspicious. It was out of character for him, and my doubts grew.

I realized that getting involved with Zack was just a way to avoid dealing with my own issues. I needed time to heal and learn to love myself, but instead, I looked for comfort in him. I was naive and too trusting, hoping he could fill the void I felt. But the truth was, I needed to find that fulfillment within myself.

Three days of complete silence went by before Zack finally called, spinning a story full of excuses for why he hadn't shown up. Then, I got a surprising call from my cousin Stacy. She told me to check Facebook, where I found a post that turned my world upside down. There was Zack, tagged in a photo, kissing another woman from his hometown in a car. I felt a rush of anger, hurt, and betrayal—I had clear proof of his cheating.

When I confronted Zack with the photo, he tried to blame the other woman. It was then I realized that letting him into my life was a mistake driven by my own selfish needs. Cheating and betrayal cut deep. They change how you see others and how you protect your own heart.

And here's the crazy part: I stayed with Zack even though I knew I should leave. I've always tried to see the good in people, but sometimes, that can blind us to the truth. One Thursday afternoon, Zack wanted to come over to talk. Against my better judgment, I let him. Standing there, listening to his apologies and promises, I got caught up in my feelings for him again.

But things weren't the same anymore. The magic was gone. After he betrayed me, I couldn't see Zack the same way. Whenever he canceled plans, claiming "family matters," I saw right through his excuses. I started making excuses to avoid seeing him, too, but that pushed him further away.

Eventually, I made the tough choice to end things. Zack stopped reaching out, and the last time he called, I actually felt relieved. I realized then that having a man wasn't what made me complete. I needed to love myself first.

I began to hold myself accountable, a hard but necessary step. I thought about my mistakes, about how I ended up in this situation. I cried and prayed for forgiveness and guidance. In that moment, I felt God's love, and peace came over me.

I've learned the hard way that loving yourself means being okay alone. It's not about needing someone else to feel whole; it's about finding that wholeness within yourself. Through this journey, I've become stronger and wiser. I know I'm not perfect, but I'm trying every day to improve with God's help.

Life's challenges teach us important lessons. Romans 2:11 reminds us that God shows no partiality—what He does for one, He can do for another. So, if you're going through tough times, remember you're not alone. God is there to help, just as He helped me.

As I close this chapter, I want to stress the importance of self-love and accountability. Our trials help us grow, and it's never too late to change. As 2 Corinthians 12:9 says, "His strength is made perfect in our weakness." So keep hope alive because there's always light at the end of the tunnel.

Activity

Healing Exercise: Rebuilding Self-Love and Accountability

Experiencing the fallout from infidelity and poor decisions can be emotionally overwhelming. This exercise is meant to guide you through these challenging emotions, help you rebuild self-love, and encourage you to take responsibility for your actions.

Materials Needed:

- Journal or paper

- Pen

- Comfortable, quiet space

Steps:

1. Reflection and Acceptance:

Take a moment to sit in a comfortable and quiet space. Close your eyes and take a few deep breaths. Reflect on the experiences you've had with infidelity or wrong choices in relationships. Accept the feelings that arise without judgment.

2. Writing Your Truth:

Open your journal or paper. Begin writing about your feelings regarding the betrayal or wrong choices you've experienced. Allow yourself to express the anger, hurt, disappointment, and any other emotions you're feeling.

3. Letter to the Person or Situation - Releasing Anger and Closure:

Write a letter to the person involved or the situation that caused you pain, expressing all the anger and hurt their actions caused you. Be raw and honest in your words. Then, when you're ready, write a paragraph about forgiving them. This forgiveness isn't about excusing their behavior but freeing yourself from the weight of anger.

4. Affirmations of Self-Love:

Write down five affirmations that focus on self-love and worthiness. Some examples include:

- "I am worthy of genuine love and respect."

- "I deserve to be treated with honesty and loyalty."

- "I am whole and complete within myself."

- "I choose to release the pain of the past and embrace my future with love."

- "I trust myself to make decisions that honor my well-being."

5. Setting Boundaries:

Reflect on the boundaries you want to set for future relationships or situations. Write down at least three boundaries that are important to you. For example:

- "I will not tolerate dishonesty or betrayal in any form."

- "I will prioritize my well-being and not compromise my values for someone else."

- "I will communicate my needs and expectations clearly in all relationships."

6. Prayer or Meditation:

Take a moment to pray or meditate on finding peace and strength within yourself. Ask for guidance and clarity as you navigate through the aftermath of this experience. Allow yourself to feel supported by a higher power or your inner strength.

Reflective Questions:

1. *What were the warning signs that something wasn't right in my past relationship or situation? How can I use these signs to trust my intuition in the future?*

2. *How did staying in this relationship or situation impact my sense of self-worth and value? In what ways can I rebuild my self-esteem and belief in my worthiness?*

3. *What actions can I take to hold myself accountable for my role in this relationship or situation? How can I learn from this experience and make healthier choices moving forward?*

4. *How can I practice forgiveness towards myself for staying in a situation that didn't honor my well-being? What steps can I take to release any guilt or shame?*

5. *How can I nurture self-love and prioritize my needs in future relationships or situations? What activities or practices can I incorporate into my life to strengthen my sense of self?*

Remember, healing is a journey, and taking it one step at a time is okay. Allow yourself the space and time to process these emotions and grow from this experience. You deserve love, respect, and happiness, starting with the love you give yourself.

"

You have within you, right now, everything you need to deal with whatever the world can throw at you.

"

- Brian Tracy

Chapter 9

FROM BROKENNESS TO HOPE

Learning to Trust Again After Betrayal

Remember that failed marriage I mentioned? After six long months apart, I was slowly getting back on my feet. The burden of a failed marriage still weighed heavily on me as I drove home in silence after dropping the kids off at school. In the driveway, looking for direction, I prayed for help fixing what was broken.

Later that day, I mustered up the courage to text my husband. To my surprise, he texted back excitedly, urging me to call. The importance of marriage really hit me; I hadn't honored my vows or God. Now, I was trying to make things right, though I knew some things might never fully heal.

After a short phone call, my husband invited me over to his place. That evening, as I arrived at his door, my heart was pounding with anticipation. He welcomed me in, and we sat on separate couches, bracing ourselves for tough talks.

Being near him felt oddly comforting and brought back a lot of memories. During our talk, I blurted out a question that had been on my mind: "Would you be okay with me and the kids moving back in?" He hesitated, but after some discussion, he said yes, though he mentioned the small space would be challenging.

Looking back, I see I rushed the decision without really thinking about how it would impact my kids. I was so focused on fixing my marriage that I didn't consider their feelings. That same day, we packed up and moved back in.

The initial excitement quickly faded as tension filled the air. My step-kids, especially my stepdaughter, clearly didn't want us there, showing it with eye rolls and sighs. My kids tried to settle in, but it was obviously strained.

Despite my husband's conflicted looks, I stayed hopeful. We went to church together, prayed as a family, and even started counseling. For a while, it seemed like things were improving.

However, my husband's lingering questions about my infidelity started to come up more and more. He wanted answers and closure, but I found myself dodging those tough conversations. I couldn't bear to think about the harm I had caused, and my avoidance only pushed him further away.

As the weeks went by, my husband became more distant and less affectionate. Our journey towards fixing things took a dark turn. It wasn't just our relationship that suffered; my children felt the strain, too. I saw changes in their behavior, especially in my oldest daughter.

One day, tensions reached a breaking point when my daughter said she wanted to leave. Overwhelmed and torn, I agreed, hoping it would bring some peace. I took her to stay with my father, trying to maintain peace while silently dealing with my own guilt.

When I got back home, the gap between my husband and my kids seemed even wider. My step-kids were treating my children poorly, and my husband didn't seem to care. I was shocked by how my kids were treated while I was gone.

Everything came to a head when my kids told me what they were going through. Seeing the sadness in their eyes broke my heart. My husband's behavior towards them was not okay, and I knew I had to make a tough decision.

That night, lying in bed, I decided to leave. I couldn't let my children suffer in such a toxic environment. The next day, I packed our bags, and we left without looking back. It was a heartbreaking decision, but putting my children first was my top priority.

In 2017, I finalized my divorce and put all my energy into rebuilding our lives. My children became my main focus, and I promised to create a safe and loving environment for them.

Life wasn't easy after the divorce, but I knew I had to keep pushing forward. In 2019, I decided to move to Desoto County for a fresh start. It was hard for my kids to leave everything they knew, but sometimes, change is needed to grow.

The transition was tough, and I often wondered if I had made the right decision. Being far from family made me feel helpless at times. But as time went on, things started to look up. I found a job at Senior Care Management Solutions, and my kids started doing better in their new school.

Throughout all this, I learned to trust in God's plan. Even when things seemed really tough, I held onto my faith. Matthew 17:20 became my mantra, reminding me that even a little faith can move mountains.

A year after we moved, as I settled into our new home, I felt truly grateful. I realized I had to step back and let God work His wonders. He guided me through the darkest times, showing me that even in chaos, there's always hope.

Life has a way of teaching us valuable lessons through tough times. Looking back, I see that every struggle and challenge has helped shape who I am today. I may not have all the answers, but I know that with faith and perseverance, I can face any challenge.

So, if you're going through hard times, remember to keep hope alive. Trust in God's plan, even when it feels like everything's against you. And remember, no matter how dark the path might seem, there's always light at the end of the tunnel.

Activity

Healing Exercise: Finding Clarity and Strength

Experiencing the aftermath of a failed marriage can be overwhelming and emotionally draining. This exercise is designed to help you navigate these feelings, find clarity, and gather the strength to move forward.

Materials Needed:

- Journal or paper

- Pen

- Comfortable, quiet space

Steps:

1. Reflection and Acceptance:

Take a moment to sit in a comfortable and quiet space. Close your eyes and take a few deep breaths. Reflect on the experiences you've had with your failed marriage. Accept the feelings that arise without judgment.

2. Writing Your Truth:

Open your journal or paper. Begin writing about your feelings regarding the failed marriage. Allow yourself to express the sadness, disappointment, anger, and other emotions you're feeling. Write freely without worrying about grammar or structure.

3. List of Learnings:

Create a list of lessons you've learned from this experience. These can be personal growth lessons, insights into relationships, or realizations about yourself. For example:

- "I've learned the importance of setting boundaries in relationships."

- "I now understand the value of effective communication in a marriage."

- "I've realized that my happiness cannot solely depend on someone else."

4. Vision Board of Future Goals:

Collect some magazines and newspapers, or print out pictures from the internet. Make a vision board of your future goals and dreams. This could feature your career goals, personal development, travel spots, hobbies you wish to explore, or anything else that inspires happiness and excitement in you. Attach these images onto a board or paper and place them where you can see them often as a motivation for what you aim to achieve.

5. Letter to Your Future Self:

Write a letter to your future self, expressing your hopes, dreams, and intentions for the future. Talk about how you envision your life moving forward, the person you want to become, and the experiences you want to have. Seal this letter in an envelope and keep it somewhere safe. Set a date in the future when you'll open it to reflect on your progress.

6. Affirmations for Strength:

Write down five affirmations that focus on strength, resilience, and self-empowerment. Some examples include:

- "I am capable of overcoming any challenge that comes my way."

- "I trust in my ability to create a bright and fulfilling future for myself."

- "I release the past and embrace the limitless possibilities of the future."

- "I am strong, resilient, and worthy of love and happiness."

- "I have the courage to create the life I desire."

7. Creating a Symbol of Release:

Choose a small object or symbol that signifies the weight of the past and the burdens you are ready to let go of. This could be a stone, a piece of paper with words written on it, or any meaningful item. Take this object outside and release it. You could bury it, toss it into water, or leave it somewhere. As you do this, imagine letting go of the burdens and starting a fresh chapter in your life.

Reflective Questions:

1. What are the most significant lessons from your failed marriage?

2. How do you envision your life moving forward now that this chapter has ended?

3. What steps can you take to prioritize your well-being and happiness in the coming months?

4. What are some goals or aspirations for your personal growth and development?

5. How can you cultivate a sense of strength and resilience as you navigate this new phase of life?

Keep in mind that healing is a journey, and it's perfectly fine to take it one step at a time. Give yourself the space and time needed to work through these emotions and learn from this experience. You possess the inner strength to build a bright and fulfilling future.

"

The greatest glory in living lies not in never falling, but in rising every time we fall.

"

- Nelson Mandela

Chapter 10

A WORK IN PROGRESS

Embracing God's Restoration and Finding Love Again

God's love is truly unending, and as I shed tears of profound gratitude, I am compelled to share with you a story filled with hope and redemption. I have been blessed to feel God's comforting presence, particularly during the most challenging periods of my life. Reflecting on Psalms 34:18, we are reminded that the Lord is near to those with broken hearts and saves those who are crushed in spirit. This scripture has been a beacon of light for me, proving that if God could transform my suffering into triumphs, He can undoubtedly work miracles in your life and in the lives of your loved ones as well.

My journey has been fraught with obstacles: I have endured physical abuse, battled depression, suffered heartbreak, faced numerous failures, and encountered moments when I felt like I was my own worst adversary. These are the deep, often concealed scars that have shaped my identity. However, through each ordeal, I have come to realize that my experiences are not solely for me to bear; they serve a greater purpose. My story is a testament meant to uplift those in need of encouragement and to remind others that amidst adversity, there is always a promise of renewal and strength in God's unwavering love.

Jeremiah 29:11 became my anchor, reminding me that God's plans for me are filled with hope and prosperity. Looking back, I see how every hardship, every painful moment, was preparing me for the great things ahead. When panic attacks overwhelmed me in 2018, it was a turning point. I cried out to God in desperation, and He listened. From that moment, I was freed from anxiety and depression, not through my own power but God's.

I share this not to boast but to inspire you. No matter how broken you feel, God can mend, heal, and transform your life. Joel 2:25 talks about restoration, about God returning what was lost. In my life, He restored my family, my happiness, and my self-esteem. Today, I stand before you as a woman who knows her value, who has found love, and who experiences the freedom that only God can give.

Life's journey isn't always easy, but it's always worth it. Proverbs 3:5-6 advises us to trust in the Lord with all our hearts, not to rely on our own understanding, and to recognize Him in all we do. This is the way to a fulfilling and purposeful life.

I am just a woman from Jackson, Mississippi, who met a man willing to look beyond her past. Robert's patience, love, and steadfast support helped me find my purpose. He became the means through which God healed my wounds and renewed my faith in love. Choosing to be with him was the best decision I've made, and now, our life together yields lasting benefits.

So, to anyone reading this, I encourage you: do not let past pains control your future. God has a plan for you, a plan full of hope and purpose. Embrace the process of becoming a better version of yourself, knowing that your mistakes do not define you. Love yourself, accept who God made you to be, and trust in His perfect plan.

As I continue on this path of healing and new beginnings, I leave you with this thought: do not let past pain obstruct your future. Embrace the freedom and grace that God offers, and strive for the life He has prepared for you. Today, I stand as a testimony to God's faithfulness and love. And I firmly believe that He can do the same for you.

Activity

Healing Exercise: Embracing Restoration and Divine Purpose

The road to restoration after a challenging past is often a journey of self-discovery, healing, and faith. This exercise is designed to help you embrace the restoration process and find clarity in your path forward.

Materials Needed:

- Journal or paper

- Pen

- Quiet, comfortable space

Steps:

1. Reflection on God's Promises:

Find a quiet space where you can sit and reflect. Take a few deep breaths and center yourself. Meditate on Psalms 34:18 and Jeremiah 29:11. Allow these verses to sink into your heart and mind, reminding you of God's closeness to the brokenhearted and His plans of prosperity for your future.

2. Writing Your Journey:

Open your journal or paper. Begin writing about your journey through challenges and heartaches. Share the moments that have shaped you, your struggles, and the victories you've experienced. This is your space to express gratitude for the restoration you've already witnessed and acknowledge the work still unfolding.

3. List of Restored Blessings:

Create a list of blessings and restorations you've experienced. These could be relationships, inner peace, a renewed sense of purpose, or other areas where you've seen God's hand at work. For example:

- "God restored my faith in love through my relationship with [partner's name]."

- "I found inner peace and healing from anxiety and depression through God's grace."

- "My family relationships have been strengthened and restored."

4. Letter to Your Younger Self:

Write a letter to your younger self, offering words of wisdom, encouragement, and comfort. Reflect on the lessons you've learned and the growth you've experienced. Share insights you wish you knew during your darkest moments. This letter is a reminder of how far you've come and the strength you've found along the way.

5. Affirmations of Divine Purpose:

Write five affirmations that speak to your divine purpose and God's plan for your life. These affirmations should inspire confidence, faith, and trust in His guiding hand. Some examples include:

- "I trust in God's plan for my life, knowing that He leads me toward prosperity and hope."

- "I am a vessel of God's love and healing, impacting those around me positively."

- "I embrace my past as a journey of growth, and I step into my future with confidence and purpose."

- "God's restoration in my life is a testament to His faithfulness and love for me."

- "I walk in the freedom and grace provided by God, knowing that my future is secure in His hands."

6. Creating a Symbol of Restoration:

Find a meaningful symbol or object that represents the restoration you've experienced. This could be a small token, a piece of jewelry, or anything significant to you. Place this symbol in a prominent place where you can see it daily as a reminder of God's faithfulness and the restoration in your life.

Reflective Questions:

1. How have you seen God's restoration and blessings unfold in your life?

2. What are some specific moments or experiences where you felt God's presence and guidance?

3. How does your past journey of challenges contribute to your present sense of purpose and direction?

4. In what ways can you continue to trust in God's plan for your future, even when faced with uncertainties?

5. How can you share your story of restoration and faith with others as a source of encouragement and hope?

Remember, the road to restoration is ongoing, and God's work in your life is a continuous process. Allow yourself the grace to embrace each step with faith and trust, knowing He is with you every step.

"

God often uses our deepest pain as the launching pad of our greatest calling.

"

- Unknown

Chapter 11

A FULL CIRCLE MOMENT

As I sit here, pen in hand, reflecting on the journey that has brought me to this moment, I am filled with gratitude and amazement. Chapter Ten is not just another page in my book; it marks a significant point—the combination of the struggles, successes, and life-changing experiences that have shaped my story.

In the beginning, I was a young girl who grew into a woman scarred by lies and heartbreak. I moved through the darkness of emotional abuse, wrestling with questions about my self-worth and purpose. Each step forward was tough, weighed down by the scars of my past. Yet, I did not realize then that these scars would turn into sources of my strength and resilience.

My path started with slowly recognizing the constraints that held me. It was about identifying the signs of emotional abuse, those quiet yet harmful moments that weakened my spirit. It was about breaking free from the toxic cycle of manipulation and control, finding the bravery to leave behind the lies and empty promises. It involved seeking support from God, friends, family, and therapists, finding comfort in shared stories and the realization that I was not alone.

Facing my emotional scars was perhaps the toughest part of this journey. It meant confronting the pain directly, allowing myself to fully experience my past. It meant accepting the anger, the sorrow, and the tears as necessary steps toward healing. Through it all, I discovered the power of forgiveness—not for my abusers, but for myself. Forgiveness became a powerful act of self-love, a way to free myself from their past influence.

Rebuilding trust was a careful process, requiring patience and bravery. It involved learning to tell the truth from lies and real love from manipulation. It was about taking small steps, cautiously testing the waters before fully diving in. Trust, I realized, was a precious gift I gave myself—a belief in my resilience, my value, and my right to a life free from abuse.

During this journey, faith became my anchor. In moments of doubt and despair, I turned to prayer, trusting in a higher power to guide me through tough times. I found comfort in the words of scripture, promises of hope and healing that resonated through the pages of my Bible. Faith was the light that guided me through the darkest times, the steadfast belief that I was not alone.

Now, here I am—a woman transformed by her experiences, a survivor who has stepped out of the shadows into the light of self-discovery and renewal. Looking back on the chapters of my life, I see how each challenge and hardship has shaped me into the person I am today. I am no longer defined by the pain of my past but empowered by the lessons I have learned along the way.

Today, I stand before you as a symbol of hope and resilience—a testament to the fact that no matter how deeply we may fall, we have the strength within us to rise again. My story is not just my own; it is shared by many who have faced abuse, deceit, and heartbreak. It is a story of overcoming adversity, of resilience in the face of despair.

For those who have endured deceit and betrayal in relationships, remember that you are worthy of love and respect. You deserve to be treated with kindness and honesty. Your past does not define you; it is just one chapter in your story—a chapter that can lead to newfound strength and wisdom.

And to those seeking hope and resilience in the face of adversity, I offer this: Believe in the power of your own story. See challenges as opportunities for growth and trust that there is a way forward, no matter how unclear it may seem. Surround yourself with love, support, and faith, and know that you are capable of overcoming anything that comes your way.

As I conclude, I want to share a story with you—a story about resilience, hope, and the powerful impact of healing through someone else's experiences.

Imagine a woman named Lily. Her story mirrors the challenges faced by many who have endured abuse and betrayal. For years, Lily was stuck in a relationship that crushed her spirit. She was constantly faced with lies, manipulation, and emotional turmoil.

Lily felt like a bird with clipped wings, powerless to escape the cage of deceit that imprisoned her. She doubted her worth, her sanity, and whether she deserved anything better. It seemed simpler to stay with the familiar pain than to step into the unknown.

But one day, something changed for Lily. It was as though a veil was lifted, allowing her to see the truth clearly. She realized that she deserved to be treated with respect, kindness, and genuine love—not the distorted version she had known for so long.

With a heart brimming with courage and a spark of hope, Lily took her first tentative step toward freedom. It wasn't easy. There were moments of doubt, fear, and even guilt for wanting a better life. But deep down, she knew she deserved more.

Lily started to extricate herself from the web of lies and manipulation. She sought support from friends, family, and a therapist who helped her through the rocky healing path. Her journey was filled with setbacks and small victories, moments of despair and glimpses of hope.

As she dealt with her emotional wounds, Lily found a deep strength within herself that she had never recognized before. She learned to forgive—not for her abuser, but for her own peace of mind. Forgiveness became a vital part of her healing process.

Gradually, Lily rebuilt her life on a foundation of self-love, resilience, and strong faith. She found joy in simple moments, rediscovered passions she had suppressed under her past burdens, and embraced her true potential.

Lily's story is a testament to the resilience of the human spirit. It reminds us that no matter how dark it gets, there's always a light at the end of the tunnel waiting to guide us back. Reflecting on her journey, I see a replay of my path to healing.

Maybe you see a bit of yourself in Lily's story. Maybe you've felt the heavy burden of lies and betrayal, the pain of a broken heart looking for comfort. If so, I want you to know you're not alone.

We've walked this path together through the good times and bad, the twists and turns of my own story. And now, as we come full circle, I have a question for you:

Where do you see yourself in this journey of healing and finding out who you are? What dreams have you put aside, waiting for the time when you feel strong enough to chase them? Can you picture a future where you're free from your past, standing tall in your newfound strength?

I'm reminded of what Maya Angelou once said, "You may face many defeats, but you must not be defeated. In fact, facing defeats might be necessary to understand who you are, what you can overcome, and how you can come out of it." Take a moment to think about that future. Let it fill you with hope and determination because that future is within your reach. It's waiting for you to take that first step, no matter how small.

As we finish this story, let's keep these words in mind, knowing that no matter what challenges we face, we have the strength to rise, heal, and find redemption. Let this chapter remind us of the power of turning pain into purpose, darkness into light, and despair into hope. And may we all have the courage to follow our paths with strong faith and resilience, knowing that the journey to redemption is always worth it.

I'm truly thankful for the lessons I've learned, the strength I've gained, and the love that has supported me. And I'm hopeful for the future—for myself, my loved ones, and everyone on their own healing journey.

May this book be a beacon for those navigating through the dark times of abuse and heartbreak, offering comfort, support, and motivation.

Remember this: You are stronger than you think, braver than you believe, and more loved than you can imagine. The road to healing isn't always easy, but it's always worth it. Embrace your story, embrace your strength, and remember, you are never alone.

"

You have to go through the worst to get to the best.

"

- Unknown

Chapter 12

EMBRACING REDEMPTION AND RESILIENCE

As I finish this book, I think back on the complex journey I've been through, full of surprises and changes. In my own story, I've dealt with deep heartbreak, sharp betrayal, and a constant search for who I am.

From the broken pieces of a failed marriage to the tangle of poor decisions I found myself caught in, my journey has been like a rollercoaster of feelings. I've hit rock bottom, had moments of weakness where I felt completely lost, and searched desperately for something better.

Yet, through all the chaos, there's a thread of resilience in my story. Despite the challenges and pain, I didn't give up. I faced my demons, dealt with my mistakes with a heavy heart, and found the strength to get back up.

The road to getting better is tough. It takes courage, deep reflection, and a readiness to face hard truths. My story is here to give hope to anyone who has gone through similar tough times. It shows that no matter how low we might fall, recovery and a fresh start are always possible.

As I close this chapter of my life, I take with me the valuable lessons I've learned. I grasp the importance of loving myself, understanding now that this is the foundation for everything else. I recognize the importance of being responsible for my actions and seeing how they affect not just me but others, too. And I value the strength that comes from faith, which guides me through the darkest times.

I hope my story encourages you to face your journey with constant courage and resilience. May it remind you that even in the darkest moments, a hint of light always leads us to a better tomorrow.

In the end, this book is not just a set of stories; it's proof of the strength of the human spirit. It's a reminder that even when we face huge challenges, we have the strength inside us to rise, heal, and welcome the new beginnings that await us.

As I close this chapter of my life, remember that life's journey isn't about dodging the storms but learning to dance in the rain. It's about embracing both the good times and the hard times, knowing that every experience shapes who we are. I'm reminded of the twisting path I've taken, filled with unexpected twists and turns. Through my own eyes, you've seen the genuine feelings of heartbreak, betrayal, and my search to understand myself better.

Now, I invite you to think about your own journey. Welcome the challenges, learn from your mistakes, and believe in the chance for a fresh start. Like me, you have the strength inside you to get past difficulties, grow, and find your way to a better place.

Throughout this journey, several key takeaways have emerged, each offering profound lessons:

1. Self-Love and Accountability: I have learned that the foundation of growth lies in loving oneself and holding oneself accountable. It is in these moments of introspection that true healing begins.

2. Faith and Perseverance: In the midst of trials, faith has been my anchor. Faith has sustained me through the darkest nights, whether through prayer or trusting in a higher plan.

3. Facing Consequences: This story does not shy away from the consequences of our actions. I have experienced firsthand the pain and turmoil that can result from wrong choices, a reminder to be mindful of the ripple effects of our decisions.

4. Redemption and New Beginnings: Despite the challenges, this journey has ultimately been one of redemption and new beginnings. I have risen from the ashes of my past, determined to create a brighter future for myself and my loved ones. It is a testament to the resilience of the human spirit and our capacity for growth.

To you, the reader, I leave this message:

Life's journey is full of challenges, but it's also a path towards growth and redemption. As you navigate your own story, may you find the courage to face your trials, the faith to guide you through tough times, and the resilience to come out stronger. Embrace your journey, learn from it, and let it shape you into the person you're meant to be.

In the end, remember it's not the challenges we face that define us, but how we overcome them. Here's to new beginnings, second chances, and the unyielding spirit within each of us. May we all find the courage to embrace our own stories, with all their twists and turns, knowing that the journey towards redemption is always worth taking.

Moving Forward:

As we part ways with this narrative, let us carry these key takeaways with us:

- Embrace self-love and practice self-care. Remember that you are worthy of love and respect.

- Hold yourself accountable for your actions and choices. Be mindful of how your decisions impact not just yourself but those around you.

- Trust in faith, even in the darkest of times. Believe that there is a plan for you, and have the courage to follow it.

- Seek redemption and new beginnings. No matter how far you may fall, know you have the strength to rise again.

"

The wound is the place where the Light enters you.

"

- Rumi

About the Author

Tekeisha Lee is a devout woman of faith, inspired by the powerful words from Isaiah 60:22, "At the right time, I the Lord will make it happen." She is a loving mother to six wonderful children and seven cherished grandchildren, finding deep joy in her family. Tekeisha proudly calls Desoto County her home, though her roots are in Jackson, MS, in the lively Oak Creek Subdivision where she grew up.

Her educational journey ended in the 9th grade at Forest Hill High School, but she didn't let that stop her. In October 2020, during the upheaval of the COVID-19 pandemic, she bravely moved from her hometown to seek new opportunities, a significant change since she had never lived anywhere else. She embraced this shift with resilience and an open heart, eager to grow in a new environment.

Tekeisha initially worked in elder care at Senior Care, but after a year, she felt a pull towards new horizons and joined T.P. Health Care in 2022. Despite her commitment, the reality of earning a modest wage in a growing economy led her to move to CCI Healthcare. Confronted with the limited job opportunities available without a college degree, Tekeisha decided to explore entrepreneurship. In February 2023, fueled by her deep faith, she resigned from CCI

Healthcare to start her own business, Keisha's Cleansing Delight LLC.

Tekeisha's life is a testament to resilience and determination. She has overcome many challenges, fears, and doubts, attributing her success to her faith in God and her belief in her capabilities. Today, she passionately shares her journey with young women, encouraging them to find their purpose and chase their dreams with grit.

Tekeisha believes that everyone has a unique purpose in life. She urges others to find their calling, confident that it will reveal the true reason for their existence. Through her business, words, and debut book, Forgiving What I Cannot Forget: Rising From the Shadows, she aims to leave a lasting legacy for her family while empowering others to do the same.

Acknowledgement

I want to express my deepest gratitude to God, who inspired the idea for this book and gave me the clarity and determination to complete it. The words from Habakkuk 2:2, "Write the vision, and make it plain on the tablets, that he who reads it may run," have guided me throughout this journey. I am profoundly thankful for the strength that my faith has provided, enabling me to share my story despite numerous challenges. Through the grace of Jesus Christ, I have overcome, and I am eternally grateful for this.

To my incredible children—Latez, Ziandra, Kishonna, Ya'keishia, Floyd, and Xavier—your constant support has been my foundation. Your encouragement, belief in me, and proud smiles have fueled my determination. I love you all deeply.

A special thank you to my dear brother, Demarcus, who was always just a phone call away. Knowing I could lean on you during this process meant the world to me. I appreciate you more than words can say.

My heartfelt thanks to Ms. Pat, my client and a blessing in my life, whose faith in me from the moment we met was steadfast. Your encouragement and love have been a guiding light. I am grateful for your presence in my life.

To my supportive colleague, Jeanie, your immediate support and promise to get a copy of my book meant so much. Thank you for standing by me.

To my cousin Ghameka, your constant encouragement and faith in my abilities never faltered. Your words of confidence were a source of strength.

To my nephew Tony, your simple yet profound encouragement to "write the book" sparked my determination. Thank you for your unwavering support.

To my parents, Wilfred and Linda, I owe everything to you. Your love, belief in me, and unwavering support have been the foundation of my journey. I love you both dearly.

To my siblings, Tekila, Wilfred Jr., and Katina, your love and support mean everything to me. Thank you for always being there.

A heartfelt appreciation to my publisher, Reea Rodney. Your unwavering support, tough love, and constructive criticism have been invaluable. I am grateful for your faith in me and your commitment to bringing my story to life. Aunt Rose, thank you for connecting me with Reea.

Reea, you have been not only an incredible publisher but also a wonderful friend and mentor. Your dedication to helping me grow and share my story has been a blessing. I appreciate your honesty and challenging me to be better. Working with you and the team at Dara Publishing has been an honor and a privilege.

In conclusion, I extend my deepest thanks to everyone who has played a part in this journey. Your support, love, and encouragement have been instrumental. This book is as much yours as it is mine, and I am forever thankful for each of you. May God bless you abundantly.

Crisis Hotline Information

As we come to the close of *"Forgetting What I Cannot Forget: Rising from the Shadows,"* I want to leave you with resources that can be your lifeline in moments of crisis. Below are important hotline numbers and brief descriptions of the services they provide:

National Domestic Violence Hotline (US)

- Hotline: 1-800-799-7233

- Text: LOVEIS to 22522

Description: Confidential support for individuals experiencing domestic abuse. Trained advocates offer assistance, safety planning, and resources for those in need.

Crisis Text Line

- Text: HOME to 741741

Description: This text-based crisis intervention service offers support for individuals experiencing any type of crisis, including relationship issues, abuse, and mental health challenges.

Childhelp National Child Abuse Hotline (US)

- Hotline: 1-800-422-4453

Description: Provides support, guidance, and intervention for children and adults impacted by child abuse. Offers crisis intervention and referrals to local services.

CDC National STD Hotline (US)

- Hotline: 1-800-232-4636

Description: Offers information, counseling, and referrals related to sexually transmitted diseases (STDs). Provides support for testing, treatment, and prevention.

National Alliance on Mental Illness (NAMI) Helpline (US)

- Helpline: 1-800-950-NAMI (6264)

Description: Connects individuals and families to mental health resources, support groups, and education programs. Offers assistance for those dealing with mental health challenges.

SAMHSA National Helpline (US)

- Helpline: 1-800-662-HELP (4357)

Description: Provides confidential support for individuals and families facing substance use disorders and mental health issues. Offers referrals to treatment facilities and support groups.

Planned Parenthood (US)

- Hotline: 1-800-230-7526

Description: Offers information on sexual health, pregnancy options, contraception, and STDs. Provides support and resources for individuals, including teenage pregnancy counseling.

Loveisrespect

- Helpline1-866-331-9474 :

Description: This hotline is specifically for young people experiencing dating abuse and domestic violence. It provides confidential support, information, and resources.

National Suicide Prevention Lifeline

- Helpline: 1-800-273-TALK (8255)

Description: While not specific to relationship issues, this hotline provides confidential support and resources for individuals in crisis or those considering suicide.

National Association of Social Workers (NASW)

- Website: www.socialworkers.org

Phone: Varies by location (check website)

Description: Professional organization for social workers. Offers a "Find a Social Worker" tool on their website to locate social workers specializing in various areas, including trauma and abuse.

American Psychological Association (APA)

- Website: www.apa.org

- Phone: Varies by location (check website)

Description: Offers resources on finding a psychologist, mental health information, and self-help tools.

Psychology Today

- Website: www.psychologytoday.com

Description: Online directory of therapists, counselors, and mental health professionals. Allows users to search for therapists based on location, specialty, and insurance.

In moments of darkness, remember that reaching out for help is a sign of strength. These hotlines are staffed with caring professionals ready to listen, provide support, and guide you to the assistance you need. You are not alone.

Thank You

Dear Esteemed Readers,

I want to express my heartfelt thanks to each of you who has journeyed through the pages of this book. Your commitment to exploring the stories, insights, and messages within these chapters means so much to me.

My deepest hope has been that this book provides comfort and support to survivors of abuse, deceit, and heartbreak. My goal was to offer guidance and inspiration for navigating the path to healing and self-discovery, highlighting the crucial role of faith in overcoming life's challenges.

If this book has touched your heart, I kindly ask for your support by leaving a review on Amazon. Your feedback will not only help others find the book but also offer me invaluable insights for my future projects.

With heartfelt appreciation,

Tefeisha Lee

www.ingramcontent.com/pod-product-compliance
Lightning Source LLC
LaVergne TN
LVHW051245080426
835513LV00016B/1751